reading aids series

HOW TO USE WISC-R SCORES

IN READING/LEARNING

DISABILITY DIAGNOSIS

Evelyn F. Searls

University of South Florida

An **ira** *Service Bulletin*

INTERNATIONAL READING ASSOCIATION
800 Barksdale Road Box 8139
Newark, Delaware 19714

Copyright 1985 by the
International Reading Association, Inc.
Library of Congress Cataloging in Publication Data

Searls, Evelyn F.
   How to use WISC-R scores in reading/learning disability diagnosis.

   (Reading aids series) (An IRA service bulletin)
   Rev. ed. of: How to use WISC scores in reading diagnosis. 1975.
   Bibliography: p.
   1. Reading—Ability testing. 2. Learning disabilities—testing 3. Wechsler intelligence scale for children.
   1. Searls, Evelyn F.   II. Title.   III. Series.   IV. Series: IRA service bulletin.
   LB 1050.46.S43   1985   372.4'3   84-29993
   ISBN 0-87207-229-0

ii

CONTENTS

The International Reading Association attempts, through its publications, to provide a forum for a wide spectrum of opinion on reading. This policy permits divergent viewpoints without assuming the endorsement of the Association. Research data on the topic covered in this volume are not available to support some of the instructional procedures recommended or common practices described. The ideas presented are for classroom teachers or school clinicians, especially those who are sometimes provided with test results but little or no help in understanding what the results might mean in terms of diagnosis and instruction.

In pointing out that the WISC-R "must be administered by trained personnel, usually a school psychologist," the author of this volume echoes an essential recommendation in the American Psychological Association's *Standards for Educational and Psychological Tests*: "The principal test users within an organization who are charged with responsibilities related to test use and interpretation (e.g., test administrators) have received training appropriate to those responsibilities" (p. 59). A second statement from the same APA publication illuminates some of the author's suggestions for follow-up instructional activities: "The manual or report form from a scoring service cannot fully prepare the user for interpreting the test. He will sometimes have to make judgments that have not been substantiated by published evidence" (p. 13).

IRA PUBLICATIONS COMMITTEE 1984-1985 Martha D. Collins, Louisiana State University, *Chair* • Janet R. Binkley, IRA • Richard L. Carner, University of Miami • Alan Crawford, California State University at Los Angeles • Nicholas P. Criscuolo, New Haven, Connecticut, Public Schools • Michael P. French, Beaver Dam, Wisconsin, Unified School District • Pearl Grubert, Protestant School Board of Greater Montreal • Jerome C. Harste, Indiana University • Nelly M. Hecker, Furman University • Douglas Inkpen, Scarborough, Ontario, Board of Education • Eleanor Ladd, University of South Carolina at Spartanburg • Donald R. Lashinger, College of William and Mary • James R. Layton, Southwest Missouri State University • John C. Manning, University of Minnesota • Ruby W. Martin, Tennessee State University • Ronald W. Mitchell, IRA • Lesley M. Morrow, Rutgers University • P. David Pearson,University of Illinois • María Elena Rodriguez, Asociación Internacional de Lectura, Buenos Aires • S. Jay Samuels, University of Minnesota • Robert Schreiner, University of Minnesota • Jennifer A. Stevenson, IRA • Sam Weintraub, State University of New York at Buffalo.

Foreword

In the Foreword to the 1975 edition of Evelyn Searls' monograph, *How to Use* WISC *Scores in Reading Diagnosis*, Constance McCullough wrote:

> For those who wish to engage in further research, this volume provides a background of existing evidence. For those who wish to take a course on the administration and interpretation of the WISC, this book offers a helpful survey and should remove some of the shock of learning the intricacies of the tests and their interrelationships. For teachers who need to know the meaning, for reading, of the psychologist's findings in the case of a given child, the clarity and helpfulness of this presentation are admirable. (p.v)

The years since the publication of this volume have witnessed the validity of Dr. McCullough's insights. Indeed, researchers, diagnosticians, clinicians, and teachers have found in Dr. Searls' work a ready reference to guide investigation, assessment, remediation, and instruction. Essentially, the book has made possible a more complete understanding of the nature of the tests of the WISC, their relationships to the reading and learning processes, and the implications of the findings. In so doing, the ultimate benefit has been to afford reading professionals a more valid and more integrated perception of the individual learner.

In introducing the 1985 edition, Searls offers two purposes for the revised monograph: 1) "to describe the WISC-R and what it measures with regard to reading/learning disability in the light of current findings," and 2) "to include a chapter summarizing the research with the WISC and WISC-R as related to reading/learning disability." Thus, two new dimensions are added in the current work, the use of the revised WISC-R (published just before the appearance of the earlier work) and the extension of the focus to include learning, as well as reading, disability.

Since the WISC-R is currently more commonly used, the benefit of that emphasis is obvious. The extension of descriptive and research information to the area of learning disability may well be the most significant contribution of the new guide. With the growth of the learning disability field and the confusion that still surrounds definitional, diagnostic, and prescriptive domains of the reading/learning disability relationships, this volume should be welcomed by professionals in both fields. If this publication serves to facilitate research, understanding, and dialogue between reading/learning disability, the disabled learner (whatever the classification) will be better served.

Finally, allow me a personal note. As a person with administrative responsibility for a diagnostic-prescriptive center for school age youngsters with reading/language disabilities and for the education of advanced graduate students to assist these learners, their teachers, and parents, I have used Dr. Searls' earlier monograph as an aid in understanding aspects of the learner and the reading/language/learning processes. More importantly, the volume makes possible the interrelation and integration of the parts to the whole so as to understand both processes and person. To do less is inadequate, for both processes and persons are best understood when individual aspects, required for analysis, are interrelated and integrated to permit holistic views.

I look forward to using this new volume to make more effective for teachers and learners what one author called in his autobiography, "the journey inward." (Dag Hammarskjold. *Markings*. New York: Alfred A. Knopf, 1974.)

Roselmina Indrisano
Boston University

Preface

This monograph was originally published in 1975 under the title, *How to Use* WISC *Scores in Reading Diagnosis*. It was based on the Wechsler Intelligence Scale for Children, published in 1949, and on the wealth of clinical and research data that had accrued through the use of the WISC for twenty-five years.

Shortly before the appearance of this monograph the revised edition of the WISC, the WISC-R, was published in 1974. Since then, numerous reports have appeared in the literature on the use of the WISC-R with reading/learning disabled children. To a great extent these reports have stemmed from work in the field of specific learning disabilities. Old insights from the use of the WISC have been confirmed, and new insights have been discovered. Therefore, my first purpose in revising this monograph was to describe the WISC-R and what it measures with regard to reading/learning disability in the light of current findings. Accordingly, the title has been changed to *How to Use* WISC-R *Scores in Reading/Learning Disability Diagnosis*. Like the original, this revision was written primarily for the use of educators (classroom teachers, reading teachers, SLD teachers) who want to go beyond the numerical values of the WISC-R IQS and understand the implications of the scores for the diagnosis and instruction of individual students.

Although written primarily for practitioners (in line with IRA's editorial policy for titles in the Reading Aids Series), the original monograph has come to be used as a supplementary text in university courses in the diagnosis of reading and learning disabilities. A number of instructors have written to ask for an expanded list of references and a fuller treatment of research findings. Hence, my second purpose for this revision was to include a chapter summarizing the research with the WISC and WISC-R as related to reading/learning disability. Chapter 6 serves this purpose.

I wish to thank The Psychological Corporation for providing examples of the types of questions and tasks to be found on the WISC-R so that the security of the test would not be violated, as it would have been if actual test items were used. As pointed out in Chapter 1, the WISC-R is a classified psychological test, and its use is limited to personnel who have had extensive training in its administration and interpretation. However, the *Standards for Educational and Psychological Tests* of the American Psychological Association (Buros, 1974) state that those who receive reports of test scores should be qualified to interpret them and that such interpretation may involve "judgments that have not been substantiated by published evidence" (p. 767). This monograph provides information to help teachers interpret WISC-R scores for their students, but because of the complexities involved in psychological testing, I encourage teachers who use this Reading Aid to consult with their school psychologist for further clarification of details not covered in this publication.

In the writing of even so brief a volume as this, there are those persons whose help made the task much easier. I want to express my appreciation to Faye R. Branca, former Professional Publications Editor of the International Reading Association. She guided the review editors and the author through the publication of the original monograph and has served very capably herself as the review editor for this revision. Finally, I want to thank my husband, V. M. Searls, a retired airline pilot and nontypist, who taught himself to use a word processor and produced an error free manuscript (well, almost!).

EFS

Chapter 1

The Individual IQ Test and Reading/Learning Disability

Overheard in a teachers' lounge: "I just got back the psychologist's report on Bill. It says he has average intelligence. If that's right, why on earth can't he read?"

Intelligence is a necessary prerequisite to the act of reading. Generally speaking, superior intelligence produces superior readers and borderline intelligence, poor readers. There are numerous exceptions to this generalization, however, particularly in the average range of intelligence. Investigators have found disabled readers and even nonreaders to have average or above average intelligence as measured on standardized intelligence (IQ) tests.

Intelligence tests are used to help determine the presence of a reading/learning disability. Jim, a sixth grade student reading at fourth grade level, may not be a disabled reader. On the other hand, his classmate, Carol, who reads at grade level, may have a reading disability. Unless we have some way to determine whether there is a discrepancy between achievement level and intellectual ability, we cannot say that a reading disability may exist (Harris & Sipay, 1980). To ascertain this discrepancy, reading diagnosticians have long advocated the use of an individually administered IQ test, because group IQ tests, requiring silent reading with good comprehension and often under timed conditions, may penalize poor readers. Furthermore, an individual IQ test is now federally mandated in the assessment of students suspected of having specific learning disabilities (*Federal Register*, December 29, 1977).

Two well constructed, reliable, and respected individual IQ tests that do not require students to read have traditionally been used—the Stanford-Binet Intelligence Scale and the Wechsler Intelligence Scale for Children (WISC) (now WISC-R since its 1974 revision). The merits of each will not be debated here. Both must be administered by trained personnel, usually a school psychologist, and both yield a global IQ that indicates a level of intellectual functioning based on how the student performed on certain tasks. Neither test measures innate intelligence, that is, an individual's inherited capacity to perform mental tasks. From the moment of birth this

1

capacity interacts with the environment; thus, only certain aspects of the results of this interaction can be measured.

In addition to a global IQ, the Wechsler Scale indicates how a student performs on verbal tasks, performance tasks, and on each separate subtest task. For this reason the WISC-R and its predecessor, the WISC, perhaps have been used more often than the Stanford-Binet in the diagnosis of reading disability. Faced with the fact that disabled readers often had global WISC/WISC-R IQs in the average range or above, investigators began to observe how poor readers scored on different tasks presented by the IQ test. Summaries of research by Strang (1968), Farr (1969), Huelsman (1970), and Sattler (1982) indicate 2 rather consistent findings: 1) Groups of disabled readers tend to score higher on the Performance than on the Verbal Scale, and 2) they tend to score lower on 5 of the subtests—Information, Arithmetic, Digit Span, Coding, and sometimes Vocabulary.

Since the majority of research with the WISC/WISC-R and reading achievement has been ex post facto (after students have been identified as disabled readers), the issue of cause and effect is still debatable. Were the poor readers inherently inadequate in certain aspects of intelligence (as tapped by the subtests on which they scored low), or had they failed to develop in these areas because of their lack of reading ability? Farr (1969) concluded from his review of the research that reading disability "negatively affects performance on intelligence tests" (p. 186).

Whether this conclusion is accepted, it becomes apparent that the global score (the WISC-R Full Scale IQ), particularly if it falls within the average range or above (according to Wechsler's classification), is probably the least important piece of information the test yields for the teacher working with the student on a daily basis. It tells the teacher that, as measured by a standardized IQ test, the student has the necessary mental abilities to learn to read; it does not give any clues as to why the student is having difficulties with the task. Too often, only the Full Scale IQ is reported to the teacher, along with comments and recommendations by the examiner. Even if the Verbal IQ, Performance IQ, and subtest scores are reported, these may have little meaning for teachers unfamiliar with the WISC-R.

The WISC-R is a classified psychological test. As such, its use is limited to personnel who have had extensive training in its administration and interpretation. This restriction is necessary in order to preserve the validity of the test. It has, however, tended to shroud the measurement of intelligence with an air of mystery. If teachers are to make maximum use of WISC-R test results as they try to remediate students' reading disabilities, they need to be knowledgeable about the test, the samples of behavior it measures, and the implications of the scores for reading diagnosis.

The purpose of this monograph is to provide such knowledge for educators (classroom teachers, reading teachers, SLD teachers) who are responsible for the planning and implementation of reading remediation. The organization and administration of the WISC-R are discussed in Chapter 2. Chapter 3 describes each subtest as to the task involved, what purportedly is being measured, method of scoring, possible implications of high and low scores, and suggested relationships to reading disability. Chapter 4 presents procedures for analyzing WISC-R scores as a means of generating hypotheses about students' cognitive strengths and weaknesses that may affect reading ability. Chapter 5 briefly describes the other two Wechsler Scales, one for young children and one for adults. Finally, for those readers who wish to delve more deeply into the research base, Chapter 6 provides an overview of the literature on the WISC / WISC-R and reading achievement.

Chapter 2

The WISC-R

The WISC-R is an individually administered intelligence test published in 1974 as a revision of the 1949 WISC. The age limits are from 6 years 0 months to 16 years 11 months, as opposed to WISC age limits of 5 years 0 months to 15 years 11 months.

The WISC-R was standardized on a sample of 100 boys and 100 girls at each of 11 age levels (6½ to 16½), a total of 2,200 children. The sample was selected to be representative of the United States population (according to 1970 census data) on the variables of race (white/nonwhite), geographic region (Northeast, North Central, South, and West), occupation of head of household, and urban/rural residence.

The change in age limits and the inclusion of a proportionate number of nonwhite children in the norming sample (not done on the WISC) are the two differences between the WISC-R and the WISC that are of major interest to readers of this monograph. Other changes were made in item content (modifying or replacing subtest items considered to be outdated, ambiguous, or unfair to particular groups) and in administration and scoring procedures. However, Wechsler (1974) intended to retain as much of the 1949 WISC as possible because of the wealth of clinical and research data that had accrued through its widespread use. Therefore, the organization of the test and the abilities it measures remain essentially unchanged.

• Organization

The WISC-R is divided into 2 parts, a Verbal Scale and a Performance Scale, each having 5 required subtests and 1 subtest usable as a supplement or an alternate.

Verbal Scale
1. Information
2. Similarities
3. Arithmetic (Timed)
4. Vocabulary
5. Comprehension

6. Digit Span (Supplement or Alternate)

Performance Scale (all timed)

7. Picture Completion
8. Picture Arrangement
9. Block Design
10. Object Assembly
11. Coding (or Mazes)
12. Mazes (Supplement or Alternate, seldom used)

It is helpful to think of these 2 scales in terms of input and output, and not as measuring different kinds of intelligence (Wechsler, 1967, 1974). The Verbal Scale involves auditory verbal input and vocal verbal output. The examiner reads aloud the questions on all subtests; the student responds orally. The Performance Scale involves visual, nonverbal input and motor, nonverbal output. Although the examiner gives brief verbal instructions for each task, the students receive visually and nonverbally the information necessary for them to perform the task, and no verbalization is necessary for the motor response.

It also should be noted that the Verbal subtests are all untimed with the exception of Arithmetic; conversely, the Performance subtests are all timed. The Arithmetic subtest and the Performance subtests are problem solving situations. Ideally, the student works rapidly, quickly sizing up the problem and starting to solve it. Excessive slowness indicates an inability to visualize the solution; excessive speed indicates impulsiveness, a lack of ability to postpone action until the solution is thought out. Therefore, timing is important on these subtests.

Ten of the subtests begin with easy items, become progressively more difficult, and are discontinued after a specified number of failed items. The 2 exceptions are Object Assembly and Coding, both on the Performance Scale. Object Assembly moves from easy to difficult, but all 4 puzzles must be attempted by the subject. Coding has 2 parts—1 intended for subjects under the age of 8 and the other for subjects age 8 or older. The subject must try to complete the appropriate part within the time limit. Chapter 3 describes each subtest in detail and explains scoring procedures.

• Administration

The WISC-R is administered by a trained examiner on a one-to-one basis to children aged 6 years 0 months to 16 years 11 months. The testing should be carried out in a quiet setting, free from distractions, and only after good rapport has been established between the examiner and the testee. It is very important for the examiner in a school setting to be known and accepted by the children to be tested and by others in their group. This may require the examiner to spend some time in the classroom getting acquainted, observing the child in the classroom situation, and establishing a friendly relationship with the teacher.

Beginning with the Information subtest, the 10 required Verbal and Performance subtests are administered in alternating order to make the testing session more interesting and varied. Wechsler (1974) placed Information and Picture Completion at the beginning because he considered them good "icebreakers" and not too taxing for the testee. If the examiner decides to include Digit Span and/or Mazes, either as alternates or supplements, they are administered at the end of the required battery.

Digit Span may be used as an alternate only if the score on any one of the other Verbal subtests has been invalidated in some way (such as an error in administration, an external interference during testing, or an unexpected emotional blocking by the testee). Mazes may always be substituted for Coding on the Performance Scale, or it may serve as an alternate for any other Performance subtest that has been invalidated. Examiners have usually preferred to administer Coding as a part of the required battery because Mazes takes longer to administer and score. When Digit Span and Mazes are used as alternates, the scores are included in the computation of the IQs.

Digit Span and Mazes always may be used as supplements, and Wechsler recommends their inclusion whenever possible because of the qualitative and diagnostic data they provide. However, when they are used as supplements, the scores are *not* included in the IQ computation.

The examiner follows explicit directions in the test manual as to what to say and do in administering the WISC-R, records all verbal responses exactly as given, and uses a stopwatch for the timed tests. Administration time may vary from 50 to 75 minutes, depending on the age of the child and the degree of elaboration of verbal responses. After the test has been administered, the examiner usually spends at least an hour making final scoring decisions, computing the IQs, and writing the psychological report.

• Reporting of Scores

Scores are recorded on the front of the WISC-R Record Form. If you have access to such a sheet for a child with whom you have worked, you may want to look at the scores as they are discussed here and in Chapter 3. Otherwise, Appendix A contains a WISC-R Record Form with data filled in.

The WISC-R yields three types of scores: Full Scale IQ, Verbal and Performance Scale IQs, and subtest scores. Wechsler (1974) uses the following terminology to classify IQs within the specified numerical ranges:

130 and above	Very Superior
120-129	Superior

110-119	High Average (Bright)
90-109	Average
80-89	Low Average (Dull)
70-79	Borderline
69 and below	Mentally Deficient

Full Scale IQ

The Full Scale IQ, if within the Average range or above, is probably the least valuable score for the teacher. There are a number of reasons for this. The first is concerned with the nature of measuring devices. All measurement is approximate. Repeated measurements of anything will vary, whether the thing being measured is a physical object, such as a table, or an intangible attribute, such as intelligence. The more exact the measuring instrument, the less variation occurs. Unfortunately, the instruments for measuring intelligence are not very exact, especially compared to those available for physical measurements. Therefore, when we consider a test score, we must take into account the margin of error.

This margin of error is known as the standard error of measurement. Suppose you repeat a certain test measurement 100 times and take the average of all the scores. That average can be thought of as the true score. You can take the range of scores which you obtain and mark the points which enclose the middle two-thirds of the scores. These points can be designated as 1 standard error of measurement above the true score and 1 standard error of measurement below the true score. You can further mark the points which enclose the middle 95 percent of all the scores that you obtain, and these points can be designated as 2 standard errors of measurement above the true score and 2 standard errors of measurement below.

Obviously, you cannot administer the same test 100 times in the school situation in order to learn the true score of the person being tested. Therefore, you need something which will give you an idea of how far away from the true score a single score may be. The standard error of measurement can be statistically computed for any test, and all reliable tests will publish the standard error of measurement in the test manual. For the WISC-R Full Scale IQ, the average standard error of measurement (across the 11 age levels) is 3.19 IQ points (Wechsler, 1974).

Now, look at the Full Scale IQ for the student with whom you have worked or for the student (John) whose scores are recorded in Appendix A. John's Full Scale IQ is 114. By subtracting and adding 1 standard error of measurement (3.19), we can say the following about his Full Scale IQ of 114. The chances are 2 out of 3 that his true IQ lies somewhere between 1 standard error of measurement below 114 and 1 standard of measurement above 114, or between 110.81 and 117.19:

```
114.00            114.00
-  3.19          +  3.19
──────           ──────
110.81            117.19
```

If we want to be more certain of the range within which his true score lies, we can subtract and add 2 standard errors of measurement (2 x 3.19 = 6.38):

```
114.00            114.00
-  6.38          +  6.38
──────           ──────
107.62            120.38
```

This enables us to say that chances are 95 in 100 that John's true Full Scale IQ lies between 107.62 and 120.38. Using Wechsler's terminology, we see that the chances are 2 out of 3 that this student has High Average intelligence, and 95 out of 100 that he has Average to Superior intelligence.

Thus, the first reason for avoiding emphasis on the Full Scale IQ is that it is at best only an approximation of the student's true IQ as measured by the WISC-R. The second reason is that situational variables may have affected the student's score. The extent of rapport between the examiner and testee, the physical setting, how the examiner feels on that particular day, how the student feels and his/her attitude toward testing—any one of these factors may cause variation of the score from the true IQ.

The last reason is that the Full Scale IQ, if within the Average range or above, does not give any clues as to why the student is having difficulty with reading. We assume that persons of Average intelligence should be able to learn to read well; why they don't is not revealed by the Full Scale IQ. Therefore, the Full Scale IQ should be considered only as an indication of the necessary cognitive abilities, or possible lack thereof, to learn to read.

Verbal and Performance Scale IQs

If considered separately, Verbal and Performance Scale IQs are subject to 2 of the same limitations as the Full Scale IQ, the margin of error and situational variables. The average standard error of measurement is 3.60 for the Verbal Scale and 4.66 for the Performance Scale (Wechsler, 1974). Thus, we must think of these IQs as falling within bands of possible scores. We can add and subtract 1 standard error of measurement to find the band within which the true score will fall 2 out of 3 times. We can add and subtract 2 standard errors of measurement to find the band within which the true score will fall 95 out of 100 times. Furthermore, any situational variables affecting the Full Scale IQ may also affect Verbal and Performance Scale IQs.

The value of the Verbal and Performance Scale IQs lies in the magnitude of the difference between them. Here the comparison is between how the students function on verbal tasks as opposed to how they function on performance tasks. A large difference (12 or more points) may indicate deficiencies in ways of processing information, in modes of expression, or in working under timed conditions, all of which also may be involved in reading disability. This will be discussed more fully in Chapter 4.

Subtest Scaled Scores

The subtest scaled scores are the most important scores the WISC-R yields for the teacher. While subject to the same limitations of error measurement and situational variables as the IQs, subtest scores may be analyzed for the intrastudent variations they may reveal. The norm mean of each subtest is 10, but more important is the student's own subtest mean on the Verbal Scale and on the Performance Scale, and how much the student varies from these means on the separate subtests of each scale. In other words, a student's performance is not compared to what others have done; it is compared to his/her own performance on the other subtests of the scale. Does the student show highs and lows in accomplishing the different tasks presented by the subtests? Glasser and Zimmerman (1967) have stated:

> As conceptualization of interpretation of test results has developed in current thinking, the notion of *level* of intelligence has become progressively less important. . . . That a youngster is of average ability may be comforting to the parent—but why can't he read? . . . What we tend to be more and more concerned with, then, is the application of what we learn of the child's cognitive and affective processes as they relate specifically to various kinds of home and classroom behavior. (p. 2)

This type of analysis tends to concentrate on the student's individual performance and is less subject to distortion by errors of measurement, administration, or test construction. How such an analysis may be made will be detailed in Chapter 4.

Chapter 3

WISC-R Subtests

In this chapter each WISC-R subtest is discussed in the order listed in Chapter 2; that is, the 6 Verbal subtests first, followed by the 6 Performance subtests. The information for each subtest includes a brief description, an illustrative question or task, the abilities measured, the method of scoring, time limits (if any), possible indications from high or low scores, and what relationship may exist between the subtest and reading disability.

The subtest information, particularly the statements regarding the abilities measured, has been compiled from a number of sources: Wechsler (1958), Glasser and Zimmerman (1967), Rapaport, Gill, and Schafer (1968), Matarazzo (1972), Kaufman (1979b), and Sattler (1982). The examples of test items are similar to those on the WISC-R but are not identical; they were supplied by the Psychological Corporation, publishers of the WISC and the WISC-R.

The possible indications from high and low scores and the relationships with reading disability have been suggested by clinicians and researchers who have worked with the WISC and WISC-R since their publication in 1949 and 1974, respectively. (See Chapter 6 for an overview of the research base.) These indications and relationships are not intended to be exclusive. They have simply been the most productive hypotheses. The perceptive teacher will find and explore other hypotheses in individual cases.

If you are looking at the scaled scores of a student with whom you have worked or at the scores in Appendix A, you can consider the norm mean of 10 as an average scaled score on each subtest, a score of 13 or above as high, and a score of 7 or below as low. However, since this compares the student to what others have done, it is not as valuable as the intrastudent comparison which will be made in Chapter 4.

• Verbal Scale

1. Information

This subtest consists of 30 questions in ascending order of difficulty. The questions are factual, requiring very brief answers (usually one to five words). These basic facts are assumed to be generally available to average American children.

Examples   "What is steam made of?"
"Who wrote *Paradise Lost?*"

What the subtest measures. The Information subtest measures long term memory of general information gained from experience and education. The subject is not required to find relationships between facts but only to demonstrate whether the student has stored these facts as general knowledge. The subtest may also measure intellectual aggressiveness or drive.

Method of scoring. Each question is scored 1 or 0, untimed; the subtest is discontinued after 5 consecutive failures.

Indications from scores. High scores may indicate a good memory, an enriched background of a high cultural level with wide reading, and/or an alertness and interest in the surrounding environment. High scores may also suggest a child who is intellectually ambitious. Low scores may indicate a poor memory, hostility to a school-type task, a tendency to give up easily, a foreign language background, and/or a culturally deprived environment. Low scores may also reflect an orientation toward nonachievement.

Relationship to reading. As stated in Chapter 1, groups of poor readers have tended to score low on 5 of the WISC-R subtests, of which Information is one. Glasser and Zimmerman (1967) stated: "Items on this subtest basically represent typical school influenced education, although it does measure more broadly based knowledge before age 7" (p. 43). Since most of the research concerned with WISC/WISC-R and reading disability has been carried out after children were identified as poor readers (usually third grade or above), the possibility exists that their inability to read well has limited their opportunities to increase their fund of general information. On the other hand, the inability to store information (poor memory) may have hindered their progress in reading. Whether the student's best learning modality is auditory or visual also may be a factor. Students who learn best through their ears rather than their eyes may have difficulty in reading (though not necessarily), but they may still accumulate information rapidly from television, films, and discussions. Thus, there have been poor readers who made average or above scores on the Information subtest, indicating that they were alert enough to pick up these facts in spite of their reading disability.

2. Similarities

This subtest consists of 17 pairs of words. On the first 4 pairs, subjects must tell one way that two objects are alike. For the remaining 13 pairs subjects must identify the similarities, either essential or superficial, among objects, substances, facts, or ideas.

Examples   "In what way are a saw and a hammer alike?"
            "In what way are a circle and a triangle alike?"

What the subtest measures. The Similarities subtest assumes that the subject has obtained facts and ideas from exposure to information both at home and at school and should be able to see essential relationships between them. The subtest thus measures long term memory, concept formation, ability to see associational relationships, and logical and abstract thinking. It also measures the ability to select and verbalize relationships between 2 concepts which seem dissimilar at first. (As the items become more difficult, the superficial dissimilarity becomes greater.)

Method of scoring. The first 4 pairs are scored 1 or 0, untimed; the remaining 13 word pairs are scored 2, 1, or 0, untimed. For the latter, 1 point is given if the subject gives a likeness at the concrete level, either descriptive ("a saw and a hammer are both made of metal and wood") or functional ("a saw and a hammer are both used to work with"). Two points are given for a more abstract likeness ("they are both tools for building"). The subtest is discontinued after 3 consecutive failures.

Indications from scores. High scores may indicate many items associated at the concrete level and/or fewer items associated at the abstract level. (Only the examiner can give this information, as the score alone will not differentiate.) The level of concept formation achieved is important since the more abstract the response, the higher the level of intelligence. Low scores may indicate an overly concrete mode of approach (subject cannot get beyond the concrete level of similarity), rigidity of thought processes (subject cannot find relationships when the 2 objects appear to be dissimilar), and/or negativism (subject insists that the objects are not alike).

Relationship to reading. Poor readers do not seem to be unduly penalized by this subtest, since they can obtain the facts and ideas necessary for concept formation in ways other than reading. Also, poor readers can get credit for the concrete level of abstraction if they are unable to function at the higher level.

3. Arithmetic

This subtest contains 18 word problems requiring mental computation (no pencil and paper allowed). The first 4 problems are to be solved using a card with a row of 12 trees; these problems are administered only to subjects under the age of 8 or those suspected of mental deficiency. Problems 1 through 15 are read aloud by the examiner. Problems 16, 17, and 18 (the most difficult) are presented on cards for the subject to read aloud before the timing begins. If the subject has a visual or reading problem, the last 3 problems also may be read aloud by the examiner.

Examples   "Sam had 3 pieces of candy and Joe gave him 4 more. How many pieces did Sam have altogether?"
"If 2 apples cost 35 cents, what will be the cost of a dozen apples?"

What the subtest measures. The Arithmetic subtest measures the ability to attend and to focus concentration in order to extract the relations involved between the numbers. *Concentration* may be defined as an "active relationship with reality," in which the individual consciously keeps out all material (cognitive and emotional) not directly pertinent to the task (Rapaport et al., 1968). The subject must be able to deal with abstract concepts of numbers and to perform the basic numerical operations of addition, subtraction, multiplication, and division. These basic operations are presented in order of difficulty so that subjects are not required to perform an operation to which they have not been exposed many times in school. Thus, the emphasis in this subtest is placed not on mathematical knowledge, per se, but on mental alertness and concentration.

Method of scoring. Each problem is scored 1 or 0 and timed separately, ranging from 30 seconds to 75 seconds per problem, depending on the difficulty. The Arithmetic subtest is discontinued after 3 consecutive failures.

Indications from scores. Glasser and Zimmerman (1967) stated: "Arithmetic is more likely than some of the subtests to reveal important clues to personality and attitudes toward school achievement. For instance, the authority dominated youngster who is eager to please may do quite well, while the resistant child who refuses even to try may do very poorly" (p. 59). Thus, high scores may indicate an obedient teacher oriented student, good concentration, and/or facility in mental arithmetic. Low scores may indicate poor attention, distractibility, anxiety over a school like task, and/or a mental block toward anything to do with mathematics. Low scores may also indicate poor school achievement because of rebellion against authority or because of cultural disadvantage. Transient emotional reactions may depress the score if the child is worried about some personal problem.

Relationship to reading. In a review of 33 reading related WISC studies, Searls (1972) found Arithmetic to be the subtest on which groups of poor readers most consistently made low scores, with 91 percent of the studies reporting this subtest significantly low. From an inspection of 30 WISC and WISC-R reading related studies, Sattler (1982) reported that disabled readers ranked lowest on the Information subtest, with Arithmetic in the next-to-lowest rank. Because Arithmetic requires the use of noncognitive functions (attention and concentration) combined with the use of cognitive functions (manipulating abstract concepts, knowledge and use of numerical operations), it may doubly penalize the poor reader. Since children are not tested when they begin school but only after they have developed a reading problem, it is impossible to tell whether reading disability has prevented their acquiring in school the knowledge necessary for success on this subtest, or whether their inability to attend and concentrate has affected learning in both areas of reading and mathematics. Farr (1969) concluded that the Information, Arithmetic, and Vocabulary subtests were probably the ones most affected by the lack of ability to broaden knowledge through reading. These 3 subtests correspond to Bannatyne's Acquired Knowledge category (1974), in which groups of learning disabled children have shown deficits (Smith et al., 1977b).

4. Vocabulary

This subtest is composed of 32 words to be identified; the words (nouns, verbs, adjectives) are arranged in order of increasing difficulty.

Examples   "What is a _____ ?"
          "What does _____ mean?"

What the subtest measures. Vocabulary is considered to be the best single verbal measure of general intelligence on the WISC-R. It measures learning ability, word knowledge acquired from experience and education, richness of ideas, kind and quality of language, and level of abstract thinking. Home background and educational opportunity can affect the score to a great extent.

Method of scoring. Each definition is scored 2, 1, or 0, untimed. A 2 point answer would be one giving a good synonym, a major use, a general classification, or a correct figurative use. Poverty of content is penalized in that 1 point is given for a vague or less pertinent synonym or minor use. The Vocabulary subtest is probably one of the most difficult to score objectively in spite of the pages of sample answers in the test manual. It is discontinued after 5 consecutive failures (responses scored 0).

Indications from scores. High scores often indicate a good family/cultural background and/or good schooling, as well as the ability to conceptualize. Low scores may indicate limited educational or family background and/or the inability to verbalize. Children from foreign language backgrounds or those from cultures where they have not been encouraged to express themselves verbally may have depressed scores.

The Vocabulary subtest may be compared to the Similarities subtest. Both measure level of abstract thinking and ability to form concepts, but the Similarities subtest is perhaps a purer measure and less likely to be depressed by reading disability. An average or above average Similarities score combined with a low Vocabulary score would suggest that the subject has the mental ability to do abstract thinking, but that opportunities to learn words have been restricted.

Relationship to reading. Research is inconclusive regarding poor readers' performances on this subtest. In some studies groups of poor readers made low Vocabulary scores, in others they did not. The determining factor may be the children's ability and opportunity to develop their vocabulary and level of conceptualization from aural rather than reading experiences.

5. Comprehension

The title of this subtest is misleading to teachers who are accustomed to thinking of comprehension as a component of the reading act. Perhaps a better title would be "Common Sense" or "Practical Judgment." The subtest is composed of 17 questions designed to find out whether children have funds of practical information which they can use to cope with and solve problems of social behavior.

> Examples   "What should you do if you see someone forget a book when leaving a seat in a restaurant?"
> "Why should you keep your money in a bank?"

What the subtest measures. This subtest measures the extent to which children have acquired the social and moral values of the major American culture through everyday living experiences both at home and at school. It also measures ability to use practical knowledge and judgment in social situations and reflects knowledge of conventional standards of behavior.

Method of scoring. Each question is scored 2, 1, or 0, depending on the degree of understanding expressed and the quality of the responses. Untimed, the subtest is discontinued after 4 consecutive failures.

Indications from scores. High scores may indicate wide experience, ability to organize knowledge, social maturity, and/or an ability to verbalize well. High scores may also indicate a child who has learned the rules of conventional behavior in our society, who knows the "right" answers, but who does not necessarily put them into practice. Low scores may indicate overdependency (failure to take personal responsibility), overly concrete thinking, inability to express ideas verbally, and/or a creative individual looking for unusual solutions. (A child whose background lies outside the major culture may be penalized since the correct answers are based on middle-class behavior standards.)

High Information/low Comprehension scores may indicate a child who is not able to synthesize and use information to solve problems. Low Information/high Comprehension scores may indicate underexposure to informative experiences.

Relationship to reading. Poor readers are usually not penalized by the Comprehension subtest, as this is the type of information which can be acquired through practical experience and oral discussion.

6. Digit Span

This subtest consists of 2 parts. The first calls for a repetition of unrelated Digits Forward beginning with a series of 3 digits and continuing through a series of 9 digits. The second part requires the repetition of unrelated Digits Backward, ranging from a series of 2 digits through a series of 8 digits.

Example   2 - 5 - 6 - 1 - 8 - 3

What the subtest measures. The Digit Span subtest measures attention span, concentration (Digits Backward), immediate auditory memory, and auditory sequencing. *Attention* may be defined as the free use of energies not specifically tied to any particular emotion, interest, or drive. These energies are at the disposal of the subject to be used in thinking and dealing with reality. Attention is both automatic and involuntary, as opposed to concentration which is conscious and voluntary (Rapaport et al., 1968).

The 2 parts of the subtest appear to be measuring different sets of skills. Digits Forward requires skill at the rote level of short term memory, whereas Digits Backward requires that the subject hold the digits slightly longer in memory and manipulate them before restating them in reverse order. Digits Backward may thus indicate flexibility, good tolerance for stress, or excellent concentration — in short, more complex cognitive processing than Digits Forward. (Whether a significant difference exists between the lengths of the forward and backward spans must be interpreted by the examiner, as the reported Digit Span subtest score does not show this.)

Method of scoring. Each subject begins with the series of 3 digits forward, repeating them after the examiner has said all 3 digits. The subject has 2 trials with each series. Two points are given if both trials are passed (all digits repeated in correct order), 1 point if one trial is passed, and 0 points if neither trial is passed. Digits Forward is discontinued after failure on both trials of any series of digits (3-9). Digits Backward is then administered, scored, and discontinued in the same manner. The scores on both parts of the subtest are added together for the total Digit Span score. The subtest is untimed as far as the subject's response is concerned, although the examiner says the digits at the rate of approximately one per second.

Indications from scores. High scores may indicate good rote memory and immediate recall, with ability to attend well in a testing situation. Low scores may indicate high anxiety in a testing situation, a possible hearing defect, disability in auditory sequencing, and/or high susceptibility to fatigue. According to Glasser and Zimmerman (1967), the most common cause of low scores has been found to be anxiety which impaired the attention span. Anxiety in the testing situation is mentioned as a possible cause of low scores on several of the WISC-R subtests. The teacher will need to confer with the examiner as to his/her observation of the student's behavior during the administration of the test, as specific test anxiety may be manifested in a variety of ways.

Glasser and Zimmerman's observation (re anxiety) was based on data from the WISC, when Digit Span was administered as the sixth subtest (at the end of the Verbal Scale). In the original edition of this monograph (based on the WISC), it was suggested that the possibility of "peak out" should be considered as a factor in low scores. The rationale was that, if the auditory verbal input of the Verbal Scale has been difficult for the subjects, students already might have passed the point of their best ability to hold and manipulate mental images without any visual aids to help. On the WISC-R, Digit Span is not administered until all 10 required subtests have been given. Although Verbal and Performance subtests are presented alternately on the WISC-R, the administration of Digit Span at the end of the testing session may now make the score particularly vulnerable to fatigue.

Digit Span may be compared to Arithmetic. Although both require the 2 noncognitive functions of attention and concentration, Digit Span relies more on attention span and Arithmetic more on concentration (Glasser & Zimmerman, 1967; Rapaport et al., 1968).

Relationship to reading. Digit Span is one of the 5 subtests on which groups of disabled readers have made low scores. In Sattler's review (1982) of 30 WISC/WISC-R studies, Digit Span was the third lowest ranked subtest for poor readers. Digit Span, together with Arithmetic and Coding, form Bannatyne's Sequential category (1974), in which groups of reading disabled children have shown deficits (Rugel, 1974). Malter (cited in Sattler, 1982) suggested that children with low Digit Span scores may have difficulty acquiring phonics skills that depend on memorization of sound/symbol relationships.

• Performance Scale

7. Picture Completion

This subtest consists of 26 drawings of objects from everyday life, each of which has an important missing element to be identified. The pictures are presented one at a time on separate cards.

Example   A picture of a dog with one leg missing. (The commercial game, "What's Missing Lotto," presents a similar task.)

What the subtest measures. Picture Arrangement measures cause/effect relationships, visual sequencing, attention to details, visual perception, and concept formation. It may also indicate social alertness and common sense.

Method of scoring. The first 4 sequences are scored 2, 1, or 0, according to success on the first or second trial. The remaining 8 picture sequences are each scored 3 points for completing the sequence in the correct arrangement, with up to 2 bonus points given for speed of response. For the last 4 sequences there are alternate arrangements that are given partial credit (2 points) but are not eligible for time bonuses. Each sequence is timed with limits ranging from 45″ to 60″. The subtest is discontinued after 3 consecutive failures.

Indications from scores. High scores may indicate alertness to detail, forethought, planning ability, logical sequential thought processes, and/or ability to synthesize parts into intelligible wholes. Low scores may indicate a problem in visual organization (sequencing), inattentiveness, anxiety, failure to use minimal cues, and/or lack of background experience with the situations depicted. The score on Picture Arrangement may be compared to that on Picture Completion, since both stress perception of details, with Picture Arrangement further requiring the logical manipulation of details. Picture Arrangement may also be compared to scores on Picture Completion together with Block Design (Subtest No. 9); all require visual perception but Picture Arrangement involves sequencing. In addition, Picture Arrangement may be compared to Object Assembly (Subtest No. 10) in that both require synthesis into wholes without a model to follow, but Picture Arrangement involves sequencing as well. Finally, the score on Picture Arrangement, when combined with the score on the Block Design subtest, provides a good nonverbal measure of general intelligence.

Relationship to reading. Poor readers do not seem to be penalized. Picture Arrangement was the second highest ranked subtest for disabled readers in Sattler's review (1982) of 30 WISC and WISC-R studies. The comic strip format is attractive and the situations presented are generally familiar to most children. While perception of details and logical sequencing are certainly abilities involved in the reading task, poor readers may succeed on this subtest because of the meaningful nature of the stimuli (Kaufman, 1979b).

9. Block Design

This subtest consists of 11 two dimensional abstract designs to be reproduced with red and white blocks (cubes). The first 2 designs are copied from a block model constructed by the examiner and are administered only to subjects under age 8 or those suspected of mental deficiency. The remaining 9 designs are reproduced from a one dimensional model (picture). The first 8 patterns utilize 4 blocks; the last 3 use 9 blocks.

Example Subjects are shown this picture on a card. They must reproduce the design with the blocks.

What the subtest measures. Block Design is considered the best single nonverbal measure of general intelligence on the WISC-R. It measures the perception, analysis, synthesis, and reproduction of abstract designs. It requires logic and reasoning to be applied to spatial relationships. It also involves nonverbal concept formation and visual-motor-spatial coordination. The subject must perceive the design on the card, analyze the component parts (making the transfer from one dimension to two dimensions), and put the parts together to reproduce the design.

Method of scoring. The first 3 designs are scored 2, 1, or 0, according to success on the first or second trial. The remaining 8 designs are scored 4 points for each pattern correctly reproduced, with up to 3 bonus points given for speed. Each design is timed with limits ranging from 45″ to 120″. The subtest is discontinued after 2 consecutive failures.

Indications from scores. High scores may indicate good conceptualizing ability, analyzing and synthesizing talents, speed and accuracy in sizing up a problem, successful use of trial and error, flexibility in problem solving, and/or excellent finger-eye coordination. Low scores may indicate a visual perception problem, poor spatial conceptualization, or a visual-motor problem.

Block Design may be compared to Object Assembly (Subtest No. 10); both measure perceptual organization and spatial visualization ability. However, in Block Design the subject uses deductive reasoning, working from the whole to the parts, while in Object Assembly the subject uses inductive reasoning, working toward the whole from the parts. Block Design provides a model; Object Assembly does not. As mentioned previously, Block Design also may be compared to Picture Completion. A low Block Design/high Picture Completion contrast may indicate adequate visual perception hampered by a visual-motor problem.

Relationship to reading. Poor readers are not necessarily penalized by this subtest. For subjects who are unable to express themselves verbally, Block Design provides a good measure of reasoning. It is also the most culturally fair of the subtests.

10. Object Assembly

This subtest has 4 jigsaw puzzles to be assembled, each of a single common object. The puzzles must be put together with no clues beyond naming the objects on the first 2 puzzles. The puzzles are progressively more difficult and all must be attempted by the subject.

Example The pieces of each puzzle are laid out in a specified manner before the subject. The number of pieces varies from 6 to 8. The pieces are not interlocking, so the subject must rely more on visualization of the whole object than on the shape of the pieces.

What the subtest measures. Object Assembly measures part/whole relationships using visual anticipation, simple assembly skills, and visual-motor-spatial coordination. The subject must work toward the whole without a model to follow and, on the last two puzzles, without any concept of the object.

Method of scoring. The Object Assembly subtest is scored as follows: 2 puzzles receive 5 points each for completion within the time limits; the other 2 receive 6 points each. If the subject correctly joins certain pieces yet does not complete the puzzle, partial credit is given. Each puzzle is timed separately, ranging from 120″ to 180″. Up to 3 bonus points may be earned for speed. There is no discontinuation point; all puzzles must be attempted.

Indications from scores. High scores may indicate experience in assembling puzzles, good motor skills, successful use of trial and error, and/or ability to visualize the whole from the parts. Low scores may indicate minimal experience in construction tasks, lack of planning ability, and/or visual perception or visual-motor deficiencies. Low scores may also indicate a highly verbal subject who lacks interest in assembly tasks.

Relationship to reading. Poor readers do not seem to be penalized. Object Assembly is gamelike and has intrinsic appeal to children. It is not difficult for children who are oriented toward concrete thinking or toward action. Subjects from low socioeconomic backgrounds often do well on this subtest because of the lack of verbal culture loading.

11. Coding

This subtest requires the subject to match and copy symbols in blank spaces provided on the test sheet. There are 2 parts, Coding A and Coding B. Coding A is for children under 8, with 45 symbols to be filled in, using a guide of symbols associated with simple shapes. Coding B is for children 8 or over, with 93 symbols to be filled in, using a guide of symbols associated with numerals. It requires the ability to use a pencil.

Examples   Coding A

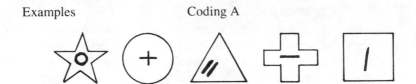

Below the guide are rows of the above shapes in random order. Subject must match the shape and write the correct symbol inside.

Coding B

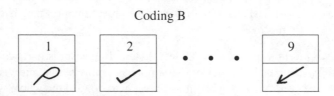

Below this guide are rows containing the numerals 1 through 9 in random order. Subject must match the numeral and write below each one the symbol associated with it.

What the subtest measures. Coding measures visual-motor dexterity and the association of meaning with a symbol. It also measures the ability to memorize quickly so that looking back at the guide is not necessary. Finally, it measures the ability to learn from visual plus kinesthetic stimuli since the subject must write down as well as look.

Method of scoring. The subtest is scored 1 point for each square correctly filled in and is timed, with 120″ allowed for completion of all squares. The subtest is all at one level of difficulty, and is not discontinued until the time limit is reached.

Indications from the scores. High scores may indicate high motivation and a great degree of concentration and sustained energy. They may also indicate visual-motor dexterity or the ability to learn new material associatively and reproduce it with speed and accuracy. Low scores may indicate specific visual defects, visual-motor coordination problems, poor pencil control, and/or disinterest in a school like task. Sometimes a low score is caused by excessive concern in reproducing the symbol exactly, thus slowing down the performance.

Relationship to reading. Coding is the only subtest on the Performance Scale on which groups of poor readers have consistently scored low. Coding was reported low in 76 percent of the WISC studies reviewed by Searls (1972). Sattler (1982) found that Coding was the fourth most difficult subtest for disabled readers on the WISC and WISC-R. (Information, Arithmetic, and Digit Span were ranked in first, second, and third place, respectively.)

Coding combined with Arithmetic and Digit Span form Bannatyne's Sequential category (1974), in which groups of reading disabled children have shown deficits (Rugel, 1974). Coding, like Arithmetic, is a timed, school like task. Furthermore, subjects must concentrate, must move their eyes quickly from the guide to the rows below, must write, and must associate meaning with a symbol. Coding also requires left-right progression. All these factors often make the task difficult for the disabled reader.

12. Mazes

This subtest consists of 9 mazes of increasing difficulty, presented one at a time. Using a pencil, subjects must draw a line showing how to find their way from the center of the maze to the exit.

Example   The mazes are similar to those found in children's commercial puzzle books.

What the subtest measures. Mazes measures planning and foresight, pencil control, and visual-motor coordination.

Method of scoring. The range of scores is from 0 to 5 points depending on the difficulty of the maze. Each maze must be completed within the time limits (ranging from 30" to 150"); otherwise, no points are given. Only one type of error is counted—entrance into a blind alley. Subjects are not penalized for lifting the pencil from the paper (as was done on the WISC), for "cutting corners," or for slight deviations from the path. However, the maze is failed (score of 0) if subjects begin drawing one-half inch or more away from the center box starting point, if they stop drawing before reaching the exit point, or if they cut through a wall to reach the goal, thereby eliminating a large portion of the maze. Illustrations are provided in the test manual to facilitate scoring decisions by the examiner. The subtest is discontinued after 2 consecutive failures (score of 0).

Indications from scores. High scores may indicate planning efficiency, ability to follow instructions, and/or good pencil control combined with speed and accuracy. Low scores may indicate inability to delay impulsive action or poor visual-motor coordination.

Relationship to reading. Because the examiner has the option of using either Coding or Mazes as the fifth subtest on the Performance Scale, and because Mazes takes longer to administer and score, this subtest has seldom been included in the test battery. Hence, no relationship to reading has been suggested.

• Summary

With the exception of Mazes, the WISC-R subtests have been researched and written about extensively in educational literature. For more detailed information about the subtests, the reader may want to consult one or more of the sources listed at the beginning of this chapter.

Chapter 4

Analysis of WISC-R Scores

If the diagnosis of a reading disability takes place in a clinical setting, the WISC-R is only one of a battery of tests utilized by reading specialists to assess the physical, emotional, and intellectual characteristics of students. In the school setting the teacher relies on direct observation of performance and behavior (considered the most valuable diagnostic tool by many authorities), use of school records, informal testing of noted skill deficiencies, and an assessment of intellectual potential whenever the latter is available. If the WISC-R is administered by school psychologists, depending on their experience and background in the field of reading education, the psychologists may be able to suggest implications from WISC-R scores as to the deficiencies that may be hindering students' progress in reading. However, psychologists are trained to interpret the WISC-R from many perspectives and from many fields of knowledge. Teachers who teach reading have more knowledge about the reading process. More importantly, they know the students with whom they work daily better than do psychologists who see students for only short periods of time.

The complexity of the reading process and the interaction of many factors in the causation of reading/learning disabilities are well established (Harris & Sipay, 1980). Many of the abilities that appear to underlie performance on the WISC-R are also involved in the reading process: auditory and visual acuity and perception, attention and concentration, short and long term memory, receptive and expressive oral language, concept formation, abstract thinking, and the ability to profit from environment and experience. Although research has identified certain characteristics of groups of poor readers, we still know very little about the ways that the mentioned abilities (and other factors such as ethnic and cultural background, parental influence, and motivation) interact to affect the reading ability of any particular individual.

The procedures suggested in this chapter encourage teachers to be detectives, using clues from their knowledge of the reading process, of students, and of the abilities measured by the WISC-R to generate hypotheses as to individuals' cognitive strengths and weaknesses that may be involved in their reading disabilities. These hypotheses can then serve as a basis for educational planning and remediation.

• Full Scale IQ

Three reasons have been advanced for avoiding emphasis on the Full Scale IQ: 1) It is at best an approximation of the student's true IQ as measured by the WISC-R; 2) situational variables may have affected the student's score; and 3) the Full Scale IQ does not give any clues as to why the student is having difficulty with reading.

It is also possible that the Full Scale IQ may be an underestimate of the cognitive abilities of disabled readers. A rather consistent pattern of low scores by groups of poor readers on certain WISC-R subtests (Information, Arithmetic, Digit Span, Coding, and sometimes Vocabulary) has emerged from summaries of research by Farr (1969), Huelsman (1970), Kaufman (1979b), and others. It follows, then (as Farr has stated very clearly), that if groups of poor readers have a Full Scale IQ in the average range, they must have scored higher on other subtests to counteract the lower scores in the subtests possibly affected by their reading disability. Kaufman (1979b) has called for research on this issue because of the possibility that "low scores on several WISC-R subtests can reasonably be attributed to poor school achievement rather than to limited cognitive ability" (p. 140). Such research, involving the routine testing of children with the WISC-R before they enter school, is not likely to be done in the near future. In the meantime, we can give reading/learning disabled children the benefit of the doubt by treating the Full Scale IQ in the following manner:

1. If the Full Scale IQ is in the Average range (90-109) or above, proceed to the analysis of Verbal and Performance Scale IQs.

2. If the Full Scale IQ is below Average, follow the psychologist's recommendations as to how the academic program may be adapted to the level of the student's ability to learn. Then proceed as in step 1.

• Verbal and Performance Scale IQs

As has been stated, the importance of these IQs lies in the possible difference between them. If the difference is large, it may indicate that the student performs better on verbal tasks than on performance tasks, or vice versa. This is particularly true if the lower IQ is the result of consistently low scores on all subtests of the scale, rather than being due to two or three very low scores on certain subtests.

1. If the numerical difference between the Verbal and Performance IQs is 11 or less, proceed to the analysis of the subtest scaled scores to see if there are high and low scores *within* each Scale that are cancelling each other. The procedures used to compute these 2 IQs may be masking

strengths and weaknesses that exist within the verbal or performance areas.

2. If the numerical difference between the Verbal and Performance IQs is 12 or more, focus on the input-output modalities of the lower score as shown in Table 1.

3. Check or recheck the following about the student where applicable.

   a. Hearing (speech reception threshold in decibels, possibility of nerve loss)
   b. Auditory perception, discrimination and sequencing
   c. Ability in verbal expression: Describe a picture, tell the events of a story, define words at reading level
   d. Vision (far point, near point, fusion, depth perception)
   e. Visual perception, discrimination, and sequencing
   f. Motor coordination of small muscles in handwriting and construction tasks

4. Generate hypotheses as to why the student's IQ was depressed on either scale.

5. Tentatively assume that the higher scale is more representative of the student's true level of functioning, then proceed to the subtest analysis.

Table 1
Processes and Modalities: WISC-R Verbal and Performance Scales

Processes	Modalities
Verbal Scale	
Input: Auditory, verbal	Auditory acuity
	Auditory perception
Output: Vocal, verbal	Verbalization
Performance Scale	
Input: Visual, nonverbal	Visual acuity
	Visual perception
Output: Motor, nonverbal	Motor coordination

• Subtest Scaled Scores

In the search for students' strengths and weaknesses, these are the most valuable scores on the WISC-R. Make certain that you receive them from the psychologist. Here, again, it is the amount of difference that matters. A

27

subtest score that differs from the student's own mean on each scale by 3 or more points is considered statistically significant (Kaufman, 1979b).

Looking for high and low scores is known as subtest profile analysis, the rationale for which is discussed in Chapter 6. The procedures will first be listed in outline form; later in this chapter they will be demonstrated with actual test scores using the WISC-R Data Sheet (Appendix B).

1. Using a list of the Verbal subtests and corresponding scaled scores, find the student's mean on these subtests and round it to the nearest whole number.

2. Determine the numerical difference between the student's mean and each subtest score. If this difference is 3 or more, write the number and the sign indicating the direction of the difference beside the subtest score. If the difference is less than 3, write only a plus or minus sign, depending on the direction. If the subtest score is the same as the mean, make no mark.

Example			
	Information	8	-3
	Similarities	15	+4
	Arithmetic	9	-
	Vocabulary	13	+
	Comprehension	11	
	Digit Span	8	-3
	Sum	6) 64	
	Mean	10.6 = 11	

3. Repeat steps 1 and 2 for the Performance subtests.

4. If the difference between the Verbal and Performance IQs is 12 or more, use the mean of the higher scale to find any additional subtests on the lower scale which are lower than this higher mean. (This assumes that the higher mean may be more representative.) As in step 2, write the minus sign and the number if the difference is 3 or more points; if less than 3, write the minus sign only.

5. Considering the tasks involved in the high and low subtests (plus or minus 3 points difference), and what each subtest purports to measure, generate hypotheses as to the student's strengths and weaknesses. (See Appendix C for a form that may be used.) Look for abilities that are common to 2 or more of the subtests. A partial list follows.

    a. Visual perception: Picture Completion, Picture Arrangement
    b. Visual-motor coordination: Coding, Mazes
    c. Visual-motor-spatial coordination: Block Design, Object Assembly

d. Attention: Digit Span, Picture Completion
e. Attention plus concentration: Arithmetic, Picture Arrangement, Coding
f. Conceptualizing ability: Information, Similarities, Vocabulary, Comprehension, Picture Arrangement, Block Design
g. School acquired knowledge: Information, Arithmetic, Vocabulary
h. Abstract thinking: Similarities, Vocabulary, Block Design
i. Sequencing ability: Digit Span, Picture Arrangement, Coding
j. Accomplishing school like tasks: Arithmetic, Coding
k. Visualizing the whole without a model: Picture Arrangement, Object Assembly
l. Short term memory: Arithmetic, Digit Span, Coding
m. Long term memory: Information, Similarities, Vocabulary, Comprehension
n. Attention to details: Picture Completion, Picture Arrangement, Object Assembly
o. Ability to profit from environment and experience: Information, Vocabulary, Comprehension, Picture Completion

6. Make comparisons between the specific subtests suggested in Chapter 3 (see Figure 1). A difference of 3 or more points between subtests is considered significant (Kaufman, 1979b). The following list is not exhaustive; other comparisons may be made by referring to subtest interpretations in Chapter 3.

a. Information versus Comprehension: Compares amount of information retained to the ability to use the information in practical situations.
b. Similarities versus Vocabulary: Both measure the level of abstraction in concept formation. Similarities is the purer measure of this, while Vocabulary indicates a wider range of learning ability.
c. Arithmetic versus Digit Span: Arithmetic relies more on Concentration and Digit Span more on attention span. A discrepancy between the 2 scores may indicate which function is giving the subject more difficulty.
d. Picture Completion versus Picture Arrangement: Both require attention to details but Picture Arrangement further requires the logical manipulation of details.
e. Picture Completion and Block Design versus Picture Arrangement: All 3 subtests require good visual perception but Picture Arrangement requires sequencing as well.

	Comprehension	Vocabulary	Digit Span	Picture Arrangement	Block Design
Information	Amount of information retained versus ability to use information				
Similarities		Level of concept formation plus range of learning ability			
Arithmetic			Concentration versus attention		
Picture Completion				Attention to details plus manipulation of details	
Picture Completion and Block Design				Visual perception plus visual sequencing	
Object Assembly				Inductive reasoning plus sequencing	
Picture Completion					Visual perception plus visual-motor-spatial coordination
Object Assembly					Inductive reasoning versus deductive reasoning

Figure 1. Comparisons between specific subtests.

f. Object Assembly versus Picture Arrangement: Both involve inductive reasoning (working with parts toward an unknown whole). In addition, Picture Arrangement involves sequencing.

g. Picture Completion versus Block Design: Both require good visual perception but Block Design involves reproduction of designs by visual-motor means.

h. Object Assembly versus Block Design: Both measure perceptual organization and spatial visualization ability. However, in Block Design the subject uses deductive reasoning, working from the whole to the parts and back again to the whole, using a model. In Object Assembly the subject uses inductive reasoning, working toward the whole from the parts without having a model.

• Demonstration of Analysis Procedures with Actual Test Scores

When the examiner who administers the wisc-r writes the psychological report, she/he may or may not include the specific test scores. Providing the examiner with a data sheet in advance is a good way to get the information you need. The wisc-r Data Sheet in Appendix B may be used for this purpose. In the following discussion the analysis procedures will be demonstrated, using actual test scores entered on the wisc-r Data Sheet in Figure 2.

Full Scale IQ

The Full Scale IQ is 126, falling within Wechsler's "Superior" classification. This girl clearly has the mental ability to learn to read and read well. Yet she was reading 2 years below grade level.

Verbal and Performance IQS

The difference between the Verbal and Performance IQs is 17, with the Performance IQ the lower. This scale relies heavily on the visual modality, so the student may need further tests of visual acuity and perception. The scale also relies on visual-motor coordination. Additional evidence needed would be handwriting samples and information as to how the student performs on construction tasks. In addition, all Performance subtests are timed. The question should be raised as to whether the pressure of time limits caused anxiety or hurried movements which affected the scores. We need to know how well Jill performs under untimed conditions. However, before pursuing these hypotheses, we will look at the subtest scaled scores to see if the lower Performance IQ is the result of lower scores on all Performance subtests or only certain ones.

Name of Subject _Jill W._   Age _10-5_ Date _10/24/83_

Examiner _Searls_   Sex _F_   Grade _5_

Full Scale IQ _126_   Wechsler Classification of Intelligence

Verbal IQ _131_   _Superior_

Performance IQ _114_   Difference between V and P IQs _17_

SUBTEST SCALED SCORES

Verbal Scale		Diff. from Scale Mean (14)	Lower than Higher Mean
1. Information	_16_	+	
2. Similarities	_16_	+	
3. Arithmetic	_10_	-4	
4. Vocabulary	_16_	+	
5. Comprehension	_17_	+3	
6. Digit Span (Supplement)	_7_	-7	
Sum of Verbal Tests	6) _82_		
Verbal Mean	_13.6 = 14_		

Performance Scale			(12)
7. Picture Completion	_15_	+3	
8. Picture Arrangement	_10_	—	-4
9. Block Design	_15_	+3	
10. Object Assembly	_12_		—
11. Coding	_8_	-4	
12. Mazes (Supplement)	Not Administered		
Sum of Perf. Tests	5) _60_		
Performance Mean	_12_		

Figure 2. WISC-R Data Sheet with scores entered.

Subtest Scaled Scores

Using the subtest scores provided by the psychologist, we compute the sum of the Verbal tests and find the mean by dividing by 6, the number of subtests administered on the scale. (Note that, although Digit Span is a supplementary test not used in determining the Verbal IQ, it *is* included in profile analysis.) The Verbal subtest mean is 14. Jill scored 3 points above this mean on Comprehension, 4 points below on Arithmetic, and 7 points below on Digit Span. These differences of 3 or more points are significant ones. On the other 3 subtests (Information, Similarities, and Vocabulary), she scored above her mean, but not significantly, so we use only a plus sign on these.

The mean of the Performance subtests is 12. Jill scored 3 points above this mean on Picture Completion and Block Design, and 4 points below on Coding. She scored below her mean on Picture Arrangement, but not significantly, so we use only a minus sign. Her score on Object Assembly was the same as the mean so no notation is necessary in the Difference column.

Since the difference between Verbal and Performance IQs was more than 12, and the Verbal IQ was the higher, we look again at the Performance subtests in relation to this higher mean. We find that on Picture Arrangement Jill scored 4 points below the Verbal mean of 14; on Object Assembly her score was below the Verbal mean but not significantly so.

Looking for Strengths and Weaknesses

In order to generate hypotheses about Jill's strengths and weaknesses, we can use a worksheet, Abilities Measured by Two or More WISC-R Subtests, as illustrated in Figure 3. (See Appendix C for a copy of the worksheet which may be duplicated.) Taking the subtests one by one, we enter the differences noted on the WISC-R Data Sheet. The Information column has plus signs, the Similarities column has plus signs, the Arithmetic column has -4 in each space, etc.

Then, we consider the abilities as listed. If an ability has at least one significant plus difference (3 or more points) and pluses in the other subtests, we mark that ability with an *S* for strength. If an ability has at least one significant minus difference and minuses in the other subtests, we mark that ability with a *W* for weakness. (If an ability does not have at least one significant difference, we cannot be as sure that a strength or weakness really does exist. We would interpret such an ability as showing a tendency in one direction or the other.) Finally, on those abilities with both pluses and minuses we put a question mark, indicating that the results are conflicting and we will need to explore further.

Accordingly, Jill seems to have these strengths: Abstract thinking, long term memory, and ability to profit from environment and experience. Her

Name of Subject __Jill W.__   Date __10/24/83__

	Abilities	Verbal Scale						Performance Scale					
		I	S	A	V	C	DS	PC	PA	BD	OA	Cod	Maz
?	a. Vis-Percep							+3	-4				
	b. Vis-Mot-Coor											-4	—
?	c. Vis-Mot-Spat									+3	—		
?	d. Attention						-7	+3					
W	e. Att + Concen		-4						-4				-4
?	f. Concept Form	+	+		+	+3			-4	+3			
?	g. Sch-Acq-Knowl	+		-4	+								
S	h. Abst. Thought		+		+					+3			
W	i. Sequencing						-7		-4			-4	
W	j. Sch-Like Task		-4									-4	
W	k. Visualize Whole								-4		—		
W	l. S-T Memory		-4				-7					-4	
S	m. L-T Memory	+	+			+	+3						
?	n. Att to Details							+3	-4		—		
S	o. Environ-Exper.	+				+	+3	+3					

Note. I=Information, S=Similarities, A=Arithmetic, V=Vocabulary, C=Comprehension, DS=Digit Span, PC=Picture Completion, PA=Picture Arrangement, BD=Block Design, OA=Object Assembly, Cod=Coding, Maz=Mazes.

Figure 3. Identifying strengths and weaknesses from a student's test data.

weaknesses appear to be in these areas: attention plus concentration, sequencing, school like tasks, visualizing the whole, and short term memory. The data are conflicting in these abilities: visual perception, visual-motor-spatial coordination, attention, concept formation, school acquired knowledge, and attention to details. Next we will look at specific subtest comparisons to see what information they may provide.

Comparison of Specific Subtests

A difference of 3 or more points is considered significant (Kaufman, 1979b); differences of less than 3 points will not be discussed.
  a. Information versus Comprehension: 1 point difference.
  b. Similarities versus Vocabulary: Same score.

34

c. Arithmetic versus Digit Span: Digit Span is 3 points lower than Arithmetic. This may mean that attention span is more of a problem than concentration. However, in light of the identified weakness in attention plus concentration, we need to consider other possibilities for the discrepancy. Jill's strength in abstract thinking may have enabled her to do better on Arithmetic; also, she may have attended better to the meaningful word problems than to the nonmeaningful random digits.

d. Picture Arrangement versus Picture Completion: These 2 subtests share the ability of visual perception, where the data were conflicting. Jill was high on Picture Completion and low on Picture Arrangement (a difference of 5 points), indicating that she could perceive important visual details when that was the only task involved. When she had to use that knowledge to order events, she did not do as well.

e. Picture Completion and Block Design versus Picture Arrangement: Jill was high on both Picture Completion and Block Design (15 on each) and low on Picture Arrangement (10). Since all 3 subtests require good visual perception but Picture Arrangement requires sequencing as well, this comparison strengthens our hypothesis that Jill has a weakness in sequencing ability.

f. Object Assembly versus Picture Arrangement: 2 point difference.

g. Picture Completion versus Block Design: Same score.

h. Object Assembly versus Block Design: These 2 subtests share the ability of visual-motor-spatial coordination, another area where the data were conflicting. The 3 point difference in favor of Block Design may indicate that Jill uses deductive reasoning better than inductive reasoning.

Exploring Other Areas of Conflict

The subtest comparisons provided information about two of the abilities in which the data were conflicting: visual perception and visual-motor-spatial coordination. Before we generate our final hypotheses, we need to look at the other 4 abilities in this category: attention, concept formation, school acquired knowledge, and attention to detail.

Attention is an ability shared by Digit Span and Picture Completion. Jill was low on Digit Span (-7) and high on Picture Completion (+3). Digit Span relies on the auditory modality and consists of nonmeaningful stimuli; Picture Completion relies on the visual modality and contains meaningful stimuli. Either of these differences could have affected Jill's scores.

Of the 6 subtests sharing the ability to conceptualize, Jill had a significantly low score on only 1, Picture Arrangement. On the others she scored above her mean. Since there are indications that the sequencing involved in Picture Arrangement may have affected that score, it would appear that Jill really has a strength in concept formation.

School acquired knowledge is based on the Information, Arithmetic, and Vocabulary subtests. Jill was low only on Arithmetic. Because Arithmetic is the only timed test of the 3, there is a possibility that the pressure of time limits had an effect. We need to know Jill's achievement level in mathematics and performance in daily work before any conclusions can be reached.

Attention to details is an ability shared by Picture Completion, Picture Arrangement, and Object Assembly. Jill scored high on Picture Completion but low on the other 2. Picture Completion requires only the identification of an important missing detail. The other 2 require the ability to visualize the whole without a model and to use details to construct the whole. It may be that the complexity of the task plus the pressure of the time limits affected Jill's ability to attend to details on Picture Arrangement and Object Assembly.

Hypotheses and Recommendations

If Jill's teacher had made this analysis of her WISC-R scores, the teacher would have had much other valuable information on hand: knowledge of Jill's home background, of how she performs and behaves in the classroom, and specific skill deficiencies. Information from all sources should be used in generating hypotheses about strengths and weaknesses and in planning remedial work. If the information from the WISC-R conflicts with the teacher's observations, greater weight should be given to the latter. We must always remember that standardized test scores are only samples of behavior at one point in time under fixed conditions. In any case, our conclusions should be tentative, subject to confirmation, modification, or rejection as further information is gained from additional testing and work with the student.

Hypothesis 1. Jill may have a vision problem. Her vision should be screened with the telebinocular and, if the results so indicate, referred to an eye specialist for a complete eye examination. Particular attention should be paid to possible near point vision problems.

Hypothesis 2. Jill has well developed verbal skills. She should be told that she has the ability to learn to read well. In the meantime the teacher can capitalize on Jill's strengths in abstract thinking, conceptualization, and long term memory by asking her to watch a film, filmstrip, or television program in an area of interest and to report to the class. She can thus acquire information and share it at a conceptual level far above that of the material she is presently able to read.

Hypothesis 3. Jill appears to have difficulty with attention and concentration, particularly in the visual modality. Harris and Sipay (1980) have made the following recommendations:

a. Check eyesight.

b. Check general physical condition, especially susceptibility to fatigue.

c. Be sure that reading materials are at Instructional Level (student knows 95 percent of the words) rather than at Frustration Level (student knows less than 90 percent of the words).

d. Supply Independent Level reading materials (student knows 99 percent of the words) commensurate with the student's interests and level of conceptualization.

e. Assign short selections to be read silently, followed by discussion of the meaning of the material. Use of prereading questions to be answered or student generated predictions to be confirmed helps to focus attention and concentration.

Hypothesis 4. Jill appears to have a problem with auditory and visual sequencing. The following activities could be used:

a. (Auditory) Decoding Morse code messages on a telegraph key made from a dry cell.

b. (Auditory) Carrying out a series of oral directions. "Please go to Ms. White's room with this message, then go to the office to get registration forms, and then go to the cafeteria for a copy of today's menu."

c. (Auditory) Repeating tongue twisters.

d. (Visual) Competing with a partner to recognize sequences of unrelated letters or numbers flashed by a tachistoscopic device.

e. (Visual) Competing with a partner to correctly sequence scrambled words to form a sentence, scrambled comic strip frames to tell a joke, or scrambled paragraphs to form a story.

f. (Visual) Constructing a graphic or pictorial story map to show the main events in a story the student has read.

Hypothesis 5. Jill performed poorly on school like tasks and may dislike them. It is natural to dislike tasks at which we have not been successful. Tutoring a younger student in reading and arithmetic would enable Jill to demonstrate her knowledge, to increase her self-esteem, and to practice with easy materials.

There are other hypotheses which could have been generated from the foregoing analysis; these 5 seem to be major ones for which there was support in the data. Further suggestions for remediation procedures applicable to specific WISC-R subtest deficiencies may be found in Jacobson and Kovalinsky (1976) and in Banas and Wills (1978). There are also many commercial reading materials which provide activities similar to those suggested.

• Summary

The analysis procedures in this chapter are intended to serve as possible ways the teacher can look at WISC-R scores in order to gather information about a student's cognitive abilities, generate hypotheses about a student's strengths and weaknesses, and plan appropriate educational intervention. It is hoped that teachers will adapt these procedures to their own purposes and perhaps develop other purposes as they become more familiar with the abilities involved in the WISC-R tasks. Here are some final reminders:

Don't think of the IQ as some mystical number to be entered forever on the student's cumulative record.

Do remember that the WISC-R, although one of the best IQ test instruments available, is still imperfect and measures only a small part of what constitutes human intelligence.

Don't forget that it is a waste of time and money to have the WISC-R administered if the results are not used or are misused.

Do become familiar with the behaviors sampled by the WISC-R and the abilities necessary to perform the tasks successfully.

Don't be satisfied with reports only of the Full Scale and Verbal and Performance IQs.

Do insist on a report of the subtest scaled scores; look for highs and lows of a student's performance.

Don't make the mistake of thinking that the WISC-R will tell you everything you need to know about the student's learning abilities; use information from all available sources.

Do carry out further informal testing as you work with the student in order to determine more specifically where the deficiencies lie.

Chapter 5

Other Wechsler Scales: WPPSI and WAIS-R

This chapter contains a brief description of the other Wechsler Scales: The Wechsler Preschool and Primary Scale of Intelligence (WPPSI, Wechsler, 1967) and the Wechsler Adult Intelligence Scale-Revised (WAIS-R, Wechsler, 1981). Because of its age range (6-0 to 16-11 years), the WISC-R is the test that teachers will encounter most often in the school setting. However, teachers who work with young children or with older adolescents may need to have some knowledge of the WPPSI and the WAIS-R.

• WPPSI

The WPPSI was published in 1967 as a downward extension (agewise) of the 1949 WISC. Covering the age range of 4 to 6½ years, the WPPSI consists of 11 subtests divided into Verbal and Performance Scales. Eight of the WPPSI subtests are downward extensions and adaptations of WISC (and WISC-R) subtests; 3 new WPPSI subtests are substitutions or replacements for 4 WISC subtests that were considered unsuitable for the younger age range. The Verbal and Performance subtests are administered in alternating order; therefore, the following list of subtests is not in the order of administration.

WPPSI Verbal Scale
1. Information
2. Vocabulary
3. Arithmetic (timed)
4. Similarities
5. Comprehension
6. Sentences (Supplement or Alternate; substitute for Digit Span)

WPPSI Performance Scale
7. Animal House (timed, substitute for Coding)
8. Picture Completion (untimed)
9. Mazes (timed)
10. Geometric Design (timed, new subtest)
11. Block Design (timed)

The Verbal Scale is very similar to that of the WISC-R. The first 3 subtests (Information, Vocabulary, and Arithmetic) appear to measure the same abilities as the parallel WISC-R subtests, except that children's knowledge at this age level will be influenced more by home and community experiences than by formal education. On the Similarities subtest, over one-half of the WPPSI questions require analogies, so the subtest may be measuring logical thinking rather than concept formation. On the WPPSI Comprehension subtest, linguistic skill and logical reasoning may influence scores more than on WISC-R Comprehension (Sattler, 1982).

The Verbal Scale supplementary subtest, Sentences, while intended as a substitution for Digit Span, does not appear to require quite the same abilities. On the WISC-R the Digit Span subtest consists of two parts calling for repetition of digits forward and backward, both presented in random order. These tasks require constant attention to the examiner. Any error in recall of a numerical sequence constitutes failure of the item. The WPPSI subtest, Sentences, requires the repetition of words in a sentence. The complete thought presented by the sentence provides an organizing principle which can help the child remember. Partial credit is given if the child remembers most of the sentence and makes only a few substitutions. Therefore, the task in Sentences would appear to be less abstract and less demanding of attention span than the corresponding WISC-R test, Digit Span.

On the WPPSI, Performance Scale 3 subtests (Picture Completion, Mazes, and Block Design) appear to measure the same underlying abilities as the corresponding WISC-R subtests. Picture Completion is not strictly timed as on the WISC-R; however, the examiner is instructed to turn to the next card if the child has made no effort to respond within 15 seconds. Mazes is a required part of the WPPSI battery rather than a supplement or alternate, as on the WISC-R. WPPSI Block Design has been made easier for younger children by the use of flat blocks (rather than cubes) and by the use of a block model from which the child works on the first 7 designs; only the last 3 designs are made from a picture model.

The Animal House subtest was substituted for WISC-R Coding as an associative learning task. However, Coding is a pencil and paper task and school like in nature, whereas Animal House is much more gamelike in its approach. It requires the child to place the correct color of disk in a board as the "house" for one of four animals pictured at the top of the board. Children often ask to "play the game again." Thus, attention and concentration, important factors in the successful completion of Coding on the WISC-R, seem to be enhanced by the motivational nature of the task on the WPPSI Animal House.

Geometric Design is the only completely new subtest on the Performance Scale of the WPPSI. The child is asked to copy 10 designs made of circles and/or straight lines. There are no time limits. It measures visual-motor-spatial coordination and nonverbal concept formation. Little emphasis is put on motor steadiness.

Because the upper age limit of the WPPSI is $6^1/_2$, there is little expectation that this test will be used much for diagnosis of reading disability. The results of a few studies suggest that WPPSI subtest profiles for good and poor readers are essentially the same (Sattler, 1982).

● **WAIS-R**

The WAIS-R was published in 1981 as a revision of the 1955 WAIS. The purpose of the revision was to update the item content where necessary and to provide new norms based on scores obtained from contemporaneous samples of the population.

The WAIS-R (for subjects age 16 years and older) is almost identical in organization, administration, and scoring to the WISC-R. It consists of two parts: a Verbal Scale with six required subtests, and a Performance Scale with five required subtests. There are no alternate or supplemental subtests. As on the WPPSI and WISC-R, the Verbal and Performance subtests are administered in alternating order; therefore, the following list of subtests is not in the order of administration.

WAIS-R Verbal Scale
   1. Information
   2. Digit Span
   3. Vocabulary
   4. Arithmetic (timed)
   5. Comprehension
   6. Similarities

WAIS-R Performance Scale (all timed)
   7. Picture Completion
   8. Picture Arrangement
   9. Block Design
   10. Object Assembly
   11. Digit Symbol (equivalent to WISC-R Coding)

The principal difference between the WISC-R and the WAIS-R is that, on the latter, Digit Span is part of the required battery, thus always included in the computation of the Verbal IQ. The subtest tasks are the same on both the WAIS-R and the WISC-R, as are the underlying abilities that the subtests measure. The procedures suggested in Chapter 4 for analyzing WISC-R scores may also be used with the WAIS-R scores of older teenagers and adults.

Chapter 6

Research: WISC/WISC-R and Reading/Learning Disability

Ever since the publication of the first Wechsler scale, there has been the hope that a qualitative analysis (i.e., looking at differences between Verbal and Performance Scales and between subtests) would reveal patterns that would enable clinicians to classify those examined into definite categories for diagnostic purposes. This hope has not been realized by researchers in the field (Sattler, 1982). Although the tests do yield much valuable information about an individual's cognitive abilities, they can not be used alone for purposes of classification. This is especially true in the area of reading/learning disability. While many studies have shown that *groups* of disabled readers have characteristic patterns of scores, attempts to identify the *individual* poor reader on the basis of these patterns have repeatedly failed. This has led many investigators to suggest that the value of qualitative analysis lies not in its possibilities for classification or categorization, but in the fact that such analysis provides clues for generating hypotheses about the strengths and weaknesses of the specific individual tested. These hypotheses must then be checked against other information about the examinee before recommendations can be made regarding necessary intervention (Kaufman, 1979b; Sattler, 1982). Investigators have consistently called for research to substantiate that certain methods of intervention (or remediation in the educational setting) are successful with individuals who have exhibited certain weaknesses. Unfortunately, this research has not been forthcoming.

The point of view expressed in this monograph has been that analysis of WISC-R scores is valuable for the insights it may reveal about individual students. The review of the literature in this chapter provides the rationale for this viewpoint under the major headings of Verbal/Performance Scale Differences and Subtest Patterns. Support from factor analytic studies as to what the scales and subtests purport to measure is presented, as well as the characteristic scores of groups of reading/learning disabled students.

The term, "reading/learning disability" has been used in this revised edition (rather than "reading disability" as in the original edition) for good reason. Much of the research during the past decade has been done in the field of specific learning disabilities. Artley (1980) proposed that reading and learning disabled mean the same thing. "A child having difficulty in learning to read or with some facet of language learning has a school learning disability — hence, is learning disabled. In the same way, because learning disabilities are manifest chiefly in reading or language areas, the same child could be said to have a reading problem" (p. 119). While it is clear that reading disabled equals learning disabled, given the importance of reading ability in the present school curricula, it is not clear that learning disabled necessarily equals reading disabled. Authorities in the field of learning disabilities are still not in agreement as to a definition acceptable to all (see feature section, "LD Definition," *Journal of Learning Disabilities*, January 1983). This lack of agreement is reflected in practice. In a recent study aimed at describing the characteristics of school aged children whom educators had identified as learning disabled, Shepard, Smith, and Vojir (1983) reported that less than one-half of a very large sample ($N=800$) exhibited characteristics consistent with definitions of learning disabilities in federal regulations and the professional literature.

The following selective review of the literature is not restricted only to those studies investigating characteristics of disabled readers. When studies of learning disabled children found WISC / WISC-R patterns similar to those identified for disabled readers, those studies were included as well.

• Verbal/Performance Scale Differences

Wechsler believed that intelligence was a global entity. He organized his tests into Verbal and Performance Scales, not because he thought they measured different kinds of intelligence, but because he hypothesized that "either through habit, training, or endowment some individuals are able to deal better with objects than with words" (Wechsler, 1958, p. 159) and that "the dichotomy is primarily a way of identifying two principal modes by which human abilities express themselves" (Wechsler, 1974, p. 9).

Factor Analytic Studies

Factor analytic studies of the WISC and WISC-R subsequently confirmed the validity of Wechsler's dichotomy. Cohen's landmark factor analytic study (1959) of the 1949 WISC standardization data at 3 age levels identified 5 factors: Verbal Comprehension 1 and 2, Perceptual Organization, Freedom from Distractibility, and a quasispecific factor. The 2 verbal comprehension factors were comprised of the 5 required Verbal subtests. Cohen noted that the distinction between these 2 factors was not sharp as there were substantial correlations between them. Three of the Performance Scale subtests loaded on the Perceptual Organization factor, the other 2 on

43

the quasispecific factor. Cohen offered no psychological interpretation for the latter factor. The Freedom from Distractibility factor was composed primarily of Arithmetic and Digit Span. Silverstein (1969) reanalyzed the same data used by Cohen, using different factoring techniques, and concluded that there were only 2 meaningful factors, represented by the Verbal and Performance Scales.

After the publication of the WISC-R, Kaufman (1975) used the computer technology then available and factor analyzed the standardization data at all 11 age levels. He found 3 factors which were similar to those found for the WISC but which lent more empirical support to Wechsler's dichotomy. Kaufman's factors were: Verbal Comprehension (all required verbal tests except Arithmetic), Perceptual Organization (5 required performance tests including Mazes but excluding Coding), and Freedom from Distractibility (Arithmetic, Digit Span and Coding). Thus, on the WISC-R the Verbal subtests without Arithmetic and the Performance subtests without Coding provide very good estimates of the individual's Verbal Comprehension and Perceptual Organization abilities. Based on Kaufman's work (1975, 1979b), Sattler (1982) proposed the following interpretation of the psychological dimensions of these 2 factors.

> The Verbal Comprehension factor score measures verbal knowledge and comprehension, knowledge obtained in part by formal education and reflecting the application of verbal skills to situations that are new to the child. The Perceptual Organization factor score is a nonverbal factor involving perceptual and organizational dimensions and reflects the ability to interpret and organize visually perceived material while working against a time limit. (p. 155)

The third factor, Freedom from Distractibility, is more difficult to interpret. It is composed of the Arithmetic subtest from the Verbal Scale, the Coding subtest from the Performance Scale, and the supplementary Verbal subtest, Digit Span. Its name indicates that it is a measure of an individual's ability to attend and concentrate. However, it may also measure numerical ability because numbers are involved in all 3 subtests. Short term memory and sequencing ability may be important components of this factor as well (Kaufman, 1975, 1979b; Sattler, 1982).

Kaufman (1981) maintained that every factor analytic study of the WISC-R had supported the construct validity of the Verbal and Performance Scales. In a number of studies by different investigators, the Verbal Comprehension and Perceptual Organization factors emerged for each age group in the standardization data, for different races and cultural groups, for both sexes, and for a variety of exceptional populations (see Kaufman, 1981, for citation of the specific studies). The emergence of the third factor was less consistent, and some investigators found more than 3 factors

(e. g., Wallbrown & Blaha, 1979). However, factor analysis is not a completely objective procedure. Even though it involves the use of statistical techniques, it is influenced by the theoretical viewpoint of the researcher and the choice of statistical methods (Matarazzo, 1972). Given this, there appears to be ample cumulative evidence to support the interpretation of the 3 factors found by Kaufman (1975).

Moreover, the third factor may be particularly important in the interpretation of the WISC-R scores of reading/learning disabled students since it is based on Arithmetic, Digit Span, and Coding, which, along with Information, are the subtests on which groups of these students have consistently made low scores. These 4 subtests have come to be known as the ACID group (Arithmetic, Coding, Information, Digit Span), an acronym credited to Swartz (1974), and will be discussed in the section on Subtest Patterns.

Interpreting Verbal/Performance Scale Differences

Wechsler (1974) suggested that a difference between Verbal and Performance Scale IQs of 15 or more points (significance at or beyond the .01 level) should be investigated. Kaufman (1979b) considered a 12-point difference (significance at the .05 level) worthy of attention because it offered the clinician more flexibility in generating hypotheses as to possible underlying causes. The 12-point difference was recommended in Chapter 4 as a starting point for the teacher's detective work. In addition to the consideration of input/output processes and modalities involved in the 2 scales (as suggested in Chapter 4), other interpretations for large Verbal/Performance Scale differences have been suggested (Kaufman, 1979b).

1. Socioeconomic level may be a factor. Analysis of the WISC-R standardization data indicated that children from professional families tended to score higher on the Verbal Scale while children of unskilled workers scored higher on Performance.

2. Bilingual and black dialect speaking children may have depressed Verbal Scale IQs.

3. The inability to work well under time pressure may depress Performance Scale IQs since all the subtests are timed.

4. Field dependence versus field independence as a cognitive style may cause differences. Field independent children have been found to score high on at least 3 subtests of the Performance Scale.

5. Dependence on one or the other cerebral hemispheres may be a factor. There is currently much interest in the "left-brain, right-brain" question, with some evidence from neuropsychological studies of significant Verbal IQ/left hemisphere and Performance IQ/right hemisphere relationships (see Kaufman, 1979a).

The first 3 of these interpretations are better supported by research and may be confirmed or rejected by a teacher by consulting other data about the child. The last 2 are still in the exploratory stage and are not likely to be of much practical use to the teacher at the present time.

Verbal/Performance Scale differences should never be interpreted without an accompanying analysis of the subtests within each scale. The summative procedures involved in the computation of the Verbal and Performance IQs may mask significant intrascale subtest differences that make Verbal/Performance Scale discrepancies meaningless for interpretive purposes (Kaufman, 1979b).

• Subtest Patterns

Subtest patterns on the WISC and WISC-R have been of interest to researchers and clinicians since the publication of the WISC in 1949. In the 25 years between the publication of the 2 tests, profile analysis, looking for high and low scores on individual subtests, was the technique most reported. This body of research on the WISC is summarized by referring to several reviews of the literature. Research on the WISC-R patterns has been primarily in terms of comparisons among Bannatyne's categories (1968, 1974). These studies are discussed individually.

WISC Patterns

Huelsman (1970) reviewed 20 studies of the WISC subtest scores of disabled readers, spanning the years 1952 to 1967. He found that 100 percent of these studies reported low scores on the Arithmetic subtest, 95 percent reported low Coding scores, 80 percent low Information scores, and 60 percent low Digit Span scores. He labeled this pattern the "WISC syndrome for disabled readers." In his own study, Huelsman found the same pattern but was unable to use it to identify individual poor readers. He suggested that one reason for this failure might be the existence of subgroups of disabled readers; the studies he reviewed had treated disabled readers as if they were all of one type. He recommended that the low subtest scores of each disabled reader should be considered individually in order to generate hypotheses with regard to needed remediation.

In an unpublished dissertation, Searls (1972) reviewed 33 WISC and reading disability studies, covering the years 1952 to 1970. She reported percentages of similar magnitude to Huelsman's. Arithmetic was low in 91 percent of the studies, Coding in 76 percent, Information in 65 percent, Digit Span in 62 percent. In spite of differences among the studies in procedure, design, size of sample, and characteristics of the sample (age, grade level, sex, bilingualism, socioeconomic level, and degree of reading retardation), Searls concluded that the WISC disabled reader syndrome was well established in the literature.

Rugel's research (1974) comparing results from 25 WISC studies was important for several reasons. It appeared the same year as the WISC-R was published, thus providing an update of WISC studies before researchers turned their attention to the WISC-R. Instead of tabulating high and low scores found in the studies, Rugel compared the scores when grouped into Bannatyne's categories. He recommended a change in the subtest membership of the Sequential category which Bannatyne (1974) later acknowledged. Rugel's research apparently provided the impetus for many subsequent WISC-R studies using Bannatyne's categories.

Bannatyne's categories (1968) were first published in an article on the diagnosis of learning disabilities in the then new *Journal of Learning Disabilities*. Based on his clinical experiences, he proposed that the following groups of subtests had more psychological meaning than the Verbal and Performance Scales.

1. Spatial category: Picture Completion, Block Design, Object Assembly.
2. Conceptual category: Comprehension, Similarities, Vocabulary.
3. Sequential category: Digit Span, Picture Arrangement, Coding.

Bannatyne suggested that comparisons of scores in these 3 categories provided much more information as to a child's deficit areas. He found in his work that Genetic Dyslexic children had higher Spatial scores (sum of the scaled scores for each subtest in the category) and lower Sequential scores, with the Conceptual scores falling in the middle. He defined Genetic Dyslexia as a "term used to describe those persons (almost always male) who exhibit a syndrome of specific linguistic skill disabilities which restrict their ability to learn to read, spell, and write as well as their full scale intelligence would indicate. . . . The condition is inherited" (Bannatyne, 1968, pp. 247-248).

In 1971 Bannatyne added a fourth category, Acquired Knowledge (scores on the Information, Arithmetic, and Vocabulary subtests), and gave his interpretation of abilities involved in each category. The Spatial group required the ability to manipulate objects in space without sequencing. The Conceptual category required the manipulation of verbal concepts; because Genetic Dyslexics could accomplish this by using their superior visual-spatial ability, they could have some success with these subtests. The Sequential category required the ability to hold sequences of auditory and visual stimuli in short term memory. The Acquired Knowledge category represented the child's ability to learn in the school situation.

Bannatyne's categories were based on research findings in the literature and his own clinical work. Rugel (1974) apparently conducted the first large scale study to justify the categorization of the WISC subtests into Bannatyne's groups. From a review of 25 published and unpublished WISC studies with disabled readers, Rugel located 22 populations for which the subtest scores could be recategorized. In spite of the fact that these populations were probably heterogeneous as to the type of disabled reader included, Rugel confirmed the pattern Bannatyne had found for Genetic Dyslexics — Spatial > Conceptual > Sequential. There were 13 populations for which scores of normal readers were available. The ranking for them was Conceptual > Spatial > Sequential, but this did not occur often enough to reach statistical significance. When individual subtest scores of disabled and normal readers in 11 populations were compared, disabled readers scored significantly lower on the same 4 subtests found by other investigators — Arithmetic, Coding, Information, Digit Span (ACID).

Rugel attributed the disabled reader's low Sequential category rank to deficits in attentional and short term memory processes. Based on a review of the factor analytic studies of the WISC and his own findings, Rugel noted that Picture Arrangement appeared to be misplaced in the Sequential category and recommended replacing it with Arithmetic, a substitution with which Bannatyne (1974) later concurred.

Thus, by the time the WISC-R was published in 1974, the ACID profile for disabled readers on the WISC was generally accepted due to the cumulative evidence from numerous studies conducted over a period of 25 years. The interested reader may locate the individual studies by referring to the references given by Huelsman (1970), Searls (1972), and Rugel (1974). There is, of course, a great deal of overlap among these references, and Searls' dissertation is unpublished. She cited seven studies not reviewed by Huelsman or Rugel. These were: Karlsen (1955), Robeck (1964), Frommelt (1964), Lerand (1966), McGraw (1966), Bean (1968), and Rainwater (1968). Three other studies not in the 3 reviews are Levine and Fuller (1972), Bush and Mattson (1973) and Fuller and Friedrich (1974-1975). By adding these 10 studies to those listed by Huelsman and Rugel and eliminating the overlap between their references, the reader will have a comprehensive list of the research on the subtest patterns of disabled readers on the WISC.

WISC-R Patterns

With the publication of the WISC-R, researchers began investigating to determine if it yielded patterns similar to those found for disabled readers on the WISC. As a result of the WISC-R factor analytic research, investigators and clinicians had more empirical support for interpreting individual subtests and small groups of subtests. Contrary to Cohen's findings (1959) on the WISC, Kaufman (1975) found most of the WISC-R subtests had unique variances of sufficient magnitude to justify the interpretation of their particular contributions to the test battery. Further analyses by Kaufman

(1979b) caused him to state that the data on WISC-R subtest specificity gave clinicians "the right to make subtest-specific interpretations for all subtests *except* Object Assembly and (at ages 9½ and above) Similarities" (p. 114). In spite of this, Kaufman recommended that, in the search for possible underlying causes of low subtest scores, the subtests should first be examined in groups according to their contribution to shared abilities. Only if this method failed to yield hypotheses as to the student's problems should clinicians interpret the individual subtests. Kaufman's recommendation thus may have influenced the increased use of Bannatyne's categories in the studies appearing after 1979.

In the WISC-R studies, the populations sampled were more often labeled learning disabled (LD) than reading disabled, although researchers examining both types of populations appeared to assume the presence of reading disability, judging by their references to the WISC studies of poor readers. In the following review, this difference in populations is noted, and the criteria for the LD classification (if reported) is stated. The studies are discussed in chronological order of publication.

Vance, Gaynor, and Coleman (1976) continued to use profile analysis, rather than Bannatyne's categories, in their investigation of the WISC-R subtest patterns of 58 children identified as learning disabled by the criteria of both Bateman and McCarthy. Scores on Arithmetic, Coding, and Information were significantly low. Digit Span was not administered, possibly because it only enters into computation of WISC-R IQs if used as an alternate. Vance et al. concluded that the 3 low scores, similar to the pattern found for reading disabled groups, were probably directly related to previous school experiences and/or attentional deficits.

In addition to looking at subtest patterns, Smith et al. (1977a) were interested in ascertaining what proportion of a large sample (N=208) of school system identified learning disabled children met the criterion of "normal" intelligence, since this criterion was the one most uniformly cited as a requisite for LD classification. They reported that 37 percent of the sample did not meet their normality criteria (WISC-R Full Scale IQ of at least 76 and either a Verbal or Performance IQ of at least 90). Nevertheless, they found both subgroups (1 above the normality cutoff and 1 below) to have the same pattern of low scores: Arithmetic, Coding, and Information. Digit Span was not administered.

Smith et al. (1977b) subsequently recategorized the scores of the same LD sample in the manner suggested by Bannatyne (1974) into Spatial, Conceptual, Sequential (minus Digit Span), and Acquired Knowledge categories. The last category has not been employed frequently in studies since its use makes the categories not discrete. Two of the 3 subtests in the Acquired Knowledge category (Vocabulary and Arithmetic) are each included in another category (Conceptual and Sequential, respectively). For the total

49

sample Smith et al. found the following pattern: Spatial > Conceptual > Sequential = Acquired Knowledge. When the scores were analyzed by the level of intelligence subgroups identified in the 1977a study, only the "high" group displayed the same significantly different rankings. For the "low" group the direction of the rankings was the same, but the only significant differences were between the Spatial and each of the other categories. For a subgroup of the "low" group classified as educable mentally retarded, the pattern was Spatial > Sequential > Conceptual > Acquired Knowledge; however, these rankings were not significantly different.

In 1978 Smith retested 161 students from this same LD sample after 7 months to determine the stability of the WISC-R subtest profiles found in the 1977a study. The pattern of low scores on Arithmetic, Coding, and Information was replicated (Smith, 1978).

McManis et al. (1978) compared the Memory for Designs, Bender-Gestalt, Trail Making Test, and WISC-R scores of average ($n = 12$) and retarded readers ($n = 12$). Profile analysis revealed low scores on Arithmetic, Coding, and Digit Span for the retarded readers when compared to the average readers. The Information subtest was also low, but the difference did not reach significance. McManis et al. concluded that their results did not support the hypothesis that minimal brain dysfunction (as inferred from visual-spatial deficits) was an underlying cause of reading disability. Rather, the "basic problem of retarded readers may lie in the area of inadequate short term memory processes and difficulty in utilizing visual-perceptual information to guide rapid motor responses sequentially" (p. 450).

Vance, Wallbrown, and Blaha (1978) attempted to determine WISC-R profiles for 104 reading disabled children through Q analysis, a factor analytic technique concerned with investigating similarities among people based on their test scores. They found 5 meaningful profiles through this procedure, and 75 percent of the children could be classified into one of the profiles. The only profile resembling those found by other investigators was labeled Distractibility, characterized by low scores on Arithmetic, Information, and Digit Span. Vance et al. promised to deal with the interpretation of the cognitive processes involved in these profiles in a later report. Instead, they described the characteristics of the children exhibiting each profile in terms of their performance on other tests and in teaching situations, and they recommended remedial strategies (Wallbrown, Vance, & Blaha, 1979). In spite of this, their work is of interest because of 2 aspects: 1) They demonstrated the importance of relating WISC-R scores to a wealth of other information about the child, and 2) for 4 of the 5 groups of children, they recommended an analytic, rather than a synthetic, approach to the teaching of word attack skills.

Miller (1980a) criticized the work of Vance and his colleagues on several grounds, although he applauded their efforts to relate test results to remediation efforts. Wallbrown, Blaha, and Vance (1980) responded to Miller's attack by providing data not included in their first report; then Miller (1980b) provided a brief rebuttal. Judging from the lack of follow-up studies based on the 5 profiles, this line of research does not appear to have had a major impact.

Vance and Singer (1979) recategorized the subtest scores of 98 school system verified LD children and found some support for the Spatial > Conceptual > Sequential pattern proposed by Bannatyne and confirmed by Smith et al. (1977b). However, the lack of clarity in Vance and Singer's report made it difficult to interpret their results.

Paal, Hesterly, and Wepfer (1979) compared the scores on both the WISC and WISC-R (test-retest interval of 5 to 8 months) of a sample of 40 students who had minimal brain dysfunction (MBD). Paal et al. used MBD as a synonym for specific learning disabilities and gave no criteria for the identification of these students, except to say that all were enrolled in a university "Therapeutic Day School" and had been "carefully diagnosed." Paal et al. found very similar subtest configurations on both tests, with the lowest subtest scores being Arithmetic, Coding, and Digit Span. They conjectured that Information was not low on either test because the students were attending a special school. Although they presented no data on recategorization scores, they concluded that their results supported Bannatyne's Spatial > Conceptual > Sequential pattern.

Stevenson (1980) chose to analyze WISC-R scores of 55 children referred to a university clinic "because of academic problems defined as skill deficits great enough to interfere significantly with educational progress" by using categories proposed by Witkin et al. (1962). Although they had different labels, these categories were identical to Bannatyne's categories (1974), except that Information was substituted for Similarities in the Conceptual category. Stevenson reported no significant differences between the Spatial and Conceptual categories for the total sample, across age levels, and across intelligence levels (below average, average, above average). However, the Sequential category (called "Attention-Concentration" by Witkin et al.) was the lowest for the total sample, for younger children, and for children of average and above average intelligence.

Three WISC-R studies using samples of reading disabled children were reported in 1980-1981. In a British journal, Moseley (1980) proposed the analysis of three groups of subtests that were identical to Bannatyne's first 3 groups (1974). Moseley labeled the categories in a slightly different manner and made no reference to Bannatyne's work. A brief description of the 2 studies conducted by Moseley indicated no significant differences between Spatial and Conceptual categories, but both were significantly higher than the Sequential category.

Moore and Wielan (1981) analyzed subtest scores for a large sample

($N=434$) of children referred to a university reading clinic for suspected reading disabilities. This sample included an unspecified number of children who were subsequently diagnosed as *not* having a reading or learning disability. Moore and Wielan reported low scores on Arithmetic, Coding, and Digit Span (Sequential category), and on Information, Arithmetic, and Vocabulary (Acquired Knowledge category), thus supporting results from previous studies with reading disabled children.

The third reading related study (Badian, 1981) continued the effort (begun by Smith et al., 1977b) to identify WISC-R subtest category patterns for subgroups of reading and learning disabled students. Although she found the most "striking" and consistent difference between good and poor readers to be the much higher percentage of poor readers scoring low in the Sequential category, Badian concluded that both level of overall intelligence and chronological age affected the category pattern.

> Among poor readers of higher IQ ($M = 105.1$) the Conceptual > Spatial > Sequential profile was almost as common as the Spatial > Conceptual > Sequential profile, and among the low IQ ($M = 89.6$) poor readers the Spatial > Sequential > Conceptual profile was most common. Older high IQ poor readers were more likely to exhibit the Spatial > Conceptual > Sequential profile, and the Conceptual factor tended to be lower than the Sequential in the oldest low IQ poor readers. (p. 114)

Three WISC-R studies using samples of learning disabled children subsequently attempted to find distinctive subgroup category patterns. Henry and Wittman (1981) examined the scores of 200 children. They randomly selected 40 students from each of 5 different special education programs: LD, full time placement; LD, resource program; emotionally disturbed; educable mentally handicapped; and gifted. All children had been classified and assigned to these groups by school district personnel. Henry and Wittman recategorized the subtest scores according to Bannatyne's categories; the Sequential category included only Arithmetic and Coding scores because Digit Span scores were not available for all students. Henry and Wittman reported that the Spatial > Conceptual > Sequential pattern was characteristic of all groups except the gifted children. The latter exhibited a Conceptual > Spatial > Sequential pattern.

Schiff, Kaufman, and Kaufman (1981) found the same category pattern for a sample of 30 learning disabled children with superior intelligence ($M = 123$) as Henry and Wittman had for their gifted group; that is, Conceptual > Spatial > Sequential. The Acquired Knowledge category was omitted from the statistical analysis because it overlapped with two other categories; however, Schiff et al. stated that scores in this category were high, averaging only slightly below the Conceptual category scores. When the subtest scores were analyzed according to Kaufman's 3 factors, the children performed at the 95th percentile on the 4 Verbal Comprehension factor subtests (Information, Similarities, Vocabulary, Comprehension), at the 80th percentile on the Perceptual Organization factor (all Performance subtests except Coding), and at the 64th percentile on the Freedom from Distractibility factor (Arithmetic, Coding, Digit Span). Thus, analysis by Bannatyne categories and by factor scores resulted in a very similar pattern of strengths and weaknesses for this sample of gifted LD children.

Finally, Ryckman and Elrod (1983) recently recategorized the WISC-R scores of 208 school system identified LD children, looking for subgroups. They found only one subgroup ($n=58$) that exhibited Bannatyne's Genetic Dyslexic pattern. For most of the children Conceptual scores were higher than Spatial scores. However, the Sequential category was the lowest for all subgroups identified.

• Summary and Conclusions

Based on an inspection of 30 WISC/WISC-R studies of heterogeneous groups of reading/learning disabled children, Sattler (1982) provided a rank order listing (from highest to lowest) of the average subtest scores:

1. Picture Completion
2. Picture Arrangement
3. Block Design
4. Object Assembly
5. Similarities
6. Comprehension
7. Vocabulary
8. Coding
9. Digit Span
10. Arithmetic
11. Information

This ranking confirms what is evident from the foregoing review of the research. Profile analysis revealed the 4 most difficult subtests (ranked 8th to 11th) to be the ACID group. Recategorization of scores, whether in terms of Bannatyne's or Witkin et al.'s categories or Kaufman's factors, consistently demonstrated that the Sequential/Attention-Concentration/Freedom from Distractibility labeled group of subtests (Coding, Digit Span, Arithmetic) was significantly lower than the other groupings. The fact that Information was a low subtest when profile analysis was used (mostly on the WISC) and not when recategorization was employed (predominantly on the WISC-R) should not be interpreted as showing a difference between the 2 tests. It may be an artifact of the 2 different methods of analysis, and/or it may mean that the underlying abilities which these subtests measure vary from group to group and within groups.

Research also makes it clear that, within the groups of children classified as having reading/learning disabilities, there are numerous subgroups. Some studies found different patterns for different ages or levels of intelligence. Research to identify specific subgroups will probably continue. However, Harris (1982) warned that there may be as many types of reading disability as there are disabled readers.

Many investigators, at least as far back as Huelsman (1970), reported failure in attempts to classify children according to their patterns of scores and recommended the study of the relationship of low subtest scores to the instructional program of individual children. Yet, no one appears to have conducted such research.

The review of the literature clearly supports the value of analyzing intrastudent variations in WISC-R subtest scores in order to generate hypotheses as to an individual student's strengths and weaknesses. Procedures for conducting such an analysis for reading/learning disabled students were outlined in Chapter 4. After the original edition of this monograph was published in 1975, Kaufman (1979b), a clinical psychologist, defended this method of analyzing subtest scores, particularly the rather liberal statistical criteria used to determine significant differences. He recommended hypothesizing a weakness in an ability shared by two or more subtests if only one of the subtest scores was significantly low and the other subtests sharing that ability were also below the child's own mean. He also felt it was practical "to delve into profiles to find support for various hypotheses from subtests that were *not* significant strengths or weaknesses, knowing that the outcome of the detective work is indeed a set of *hypotheses* and nothing more" (pp. 192-193). In other words, the worst that could happen would be that such hypotheses would have to be rejected in the face of other data about the child (from further testing, observation of classroom behavior, information from parents). The best that could happen would be that such hypotheses would be confirmed by other data and would suggest effective remedial strategies. It is hoped that perceptive teachers will combine their knowledge about the WISC-R from this monograph with their knowledge about individual children to provide more successful academic experiences for reading/learning disabled students.

References

Artley, A. S. "Learning Disabilities Versus Reading Disabilities," in C. M. McCullough (Ed.), *Inchworm, Inchworm: Persistent Problems in Reading Education*, 119-124. Newark, Delaware: International Reading Association, 1980.

Badian, N. A. "Recategorized WISC-R Scores of Disabled and Adequate Readers," *Journal of Educational Research*, 1981, 75, 109-114.

Banas, N., & Wills, I. H. *WISC-R Prescriptions*. Novato, California: Academic Therapy Publications, 1978.

Bannatyne, A. "Diagnosing Learning Disabilities and Writing Remedial Prescriptions," *Journal of Learning Disabilities,* 1968, *4,* 242-249.

Bannatyne, A. *Language, Reading and Learning Disabilities.* Springfield, Illinois: Charles C. Thomas, 1971.

Bannatyne, A. "Diagnosis: A Note on Recategorization of the WISC Scaled Scores," *Journal of Learning Disabilities,* 1974, *7,* 272-273.

Bean, W. J. "The Isolation of Some Psychometric Indices of Severe Reading Disability," *Dissertation Abstracts,* 1968, *28,* 3012A-3013A.

Buros, O. K. *Tests in Print II.* Highland Park, New Jersey: Gryphon Press, 1974.

Bush, W. J., & Mattson, B. D. "WISC Test Patterns and Underachievers," *Journal of Reading Disabilities,* 1973, *4,* 251-256.

Cohen, J. "The Factorial Structure of the WISC at Ages 7-6, 10-6, and 13-6," *Journal of Consulting Psychology,* 1959, *23,* 285-299.

Farr, R. *Reading: What Can Be Measured?* Newark, Delaware: International Reading Association, 1969.

Frommelt, L. A. "An Analysis of the WISC Profiles of Successful and Unsuccessful Readers in the Elementary School," *Dissertation Abstracts,* 1964, *25,* 2849-2850.

Fuller, G. B., & Friedrich, D. "Three Diagnostic Patterns of Reading Disabilities," *Academic Therapy,* 1974-1975, *10,* 219-231.

Glasser, A. J., & Zimmerman, I. L. *Clinical Interpretation of the Wechsler Intelligence Scale for Children.* New York: Grune & Stratton, 1967.

Harris, A. J. "How Many Kinds of Reading Disability Are There?" *Journal of Learning Disabilities,* 1982, *15,* 456-460.

Harris, A. J., & Sipay, E. R. *How to Increase Reading Ability,* seventh edition. New York: Longman, 1980.

Henry, S. A., & Wittman, R. D. "Diagnostic Implications of Bannatyne's Recategorized WISC-R Scores for Identifying Learning Disabled Children," *Journal of Learning Disabilities,* 1981, *14,* 517-520.

Huelsman, C. B., Jr. "The WISC Subtest Syndrome for Disabled Readers," *Perceptual and Motor Skills,* 1970, *30,* 535-550.

Jacobson, S., & Kovalinsky, T. *Educational Interpretation of the Wechsler Intelligence Scale for Children—Revised (WISC-R).* Linden, New Jersey: Remediation Associates, 1976.

Karlsen, B. "A Comparison of Some Educational and Psychological Characteristics of Successful and Unsuccessful Readers at the Elementary Level," *Dissertation Abstracts,* 1955, *15,* 456-457.

Kaufman, A. S. "Factor Analysis of the WISC-R at 11 Age Levels between 6½ and 16½ Years," *Journal of Consulting and Clinical Psychology,* 1975, *43,* 135-147.

Kaufman, A. S. "Cerebral Specialization and Intelligence Testing," *Journal of Research and Development in Education,* 1979a, *12* (2), 96-107.

Kaufman, A.S. *Intelligent Testing with the WISC-R.* New York: John Wiley, 1979b.

Kaufman, A.S. "The WISC-R and Learning Disabilities Assessment: State of the Art," *Journal of Learning Disabilities,* 1981, *14,* 520-526.

Lerand, L. W. "Intelligence and Reading Level of Girls," *Dissertation Abstracts,* 1966, *27,* 2137B-2138B.

Levine, M., & Fuller, G. "Psychological, Neuropsychological, and Educational Correlates of Reading Deficit," *Journal of Learning Disabilities,* 1972, *5,* 563-571.

55

Matarazzo, J. D. *Wechsler's Measurement and Appraisal of Adult Intelligence*, fifth edition. Baltimore: Williams & Wilkins, 1972.

McGraw, J. J. "A Comparison of Mean Subtest Raw Scores on the Wechsler Intelligence Scale for Children of Regular and Overachieving Readers with Underachieving Readers," *Dissertation Abstracts*, 1966, *27*, 1552A.

McManis, D. L., Figley, C., Richert, M., & Fabre, T. "Memory for Designs, Bender-Gestalt, Trail Making Test, and WISC-R Performance of Retarded and Adequate Readers," *Perceptual and Motor Skills*, 1978, *46*, 443-450.

Miller, M. "On the Attempt to Find WISC-R Profiles for Learning and Reading Disabilities: A Response to Vance, Wallbrown, and Blaha," *Journal of Learning Disabilities*, 1980a, *13*, 338-340.

Miller, M. "Final Reply from Miller," *Journal of Learning Disabilities*, 1980b, *13*, 346.

Moore, D. W., & Wieland, O. P. "WISC-R Scatter Indexes of Children Referred for Reading Diagnosis," *Journal of Learning Disabilities*, 1981, *14*, 511-514.

Moseley, D. "An Evaluation of Verbal, Spatial, and Numerical Sequencing Scores in the WISC and WISC-R, with Special Reference to Children with Reading Difficulties," *Journal of Research in Reading*, 1980, *3*, 38-51.

Paal, N., Hesterly, S. O., & Wepfer, J. W. "Comparability of the WISC and the WISC-R," *Journal of Learning Disabilities*, 1979, *12*, 348-351.

Rainwater, H. "Reading Problem Indicators among Children with Reading Problems," *Psychology*, 1968, *5*(4), 81-83.

Rapaport, D., Gill, M. M., & Schafer, R. *Diagnostic Psychological Testing*, revised edition. New York: International Universities Press, 1968.

Robeck, M. "Effects of Prolonged Reading Disability: A Preliminary Study," *Perceptual and Motor Skills*, 1964, *19*, 7-12.

Rugel, R. P. "WISC Subtest Scores of Disabled Readers: A Review with Respect to Bannatyne's Recategorization," *Journal of Learning Disabilities*, 1974, *7*, 48-55.

Ryckman, D. B., & Elrod, G. F. "Once Is Not Enough," *Journal of Learning Disabilities*, 1983, *16*, 87-89.

Sattler, J. M. *Assessment of Children's Intelligence and Special Abilities*, second edition. Boston: Allyn & Bacon, 1982.

Schiff, M. M., Kaufman, A. S., & Kaufman, N. L. "Scatter Analysis of WISC-R Profiles for Learning Disabled Children with Superior Intelligence," *Journal of Learning Disabilities*, 1981, *14*, 400-404.

Searls, E. F. "WISC and WPPSI IQs and Subtest Patterns Related to First Grade Reading Achievement," doctoral dissertation, University of Miami, 1971. *Dissertation Abstracts International*, 1972, *32*, 6225A.

Shepard, L. A., Smith, M. L., & Vojir, C. P. "Characteristics of Pupils Identified as Learning Disabled," *American Educational Research Journal*, 1983, *20*, 309-331.

Silverstein, A. B. "An Alternative Factor Analytic Solution for Wechsler's Intelligence Scales," *Educational and Psychological Measurement*, 1969, *29*, 763-767.

Smith, M. D. "Stability of WISC-R Subtest Profiles for Learning Disabled Children," *Psychology in the Schools*, 1978, *15*, 4-7.

Smith, M. D., Coleman, J.M., Dokecki, P.R., & Davis, E. "Intellectual Characteristics of School Labeled Learning Disabled Children," *Exceptional Children*, 1977a, *43*, 352-357.

Smith, M. D., Coleman, J.M., Dokecki, P.R., & Davis, E. "Recategorized WISC-R Scores of Learning Disabled Children," *Journal of Learning Disabilities, 1977b, 10,* 437-443.

Stevenson, L. P. "WISC-R Analysis: Implications for Diagnosis and Intervention," *Journal of Learning Disabilities,* 1980, *13,* 346-349.

Strang, R. *Reading Diagnosis and Remediation.* Newark, Delaware: International Reading Association, 1968.

Swartz, G. A. *The Language Learning System.* New York: Simon & Schuster, 1974.

Vance, H. B., Gaynor, P., & Coleman, M. "Analysis of Cognitive Abilities for Learning Disabled Children," *Psychology in the Schools,* 1976, *13,* 477-483.

Vance, H. B., & Singer, M. G. "Recategorization of the WISC-R Subtest Scaled Scores for Learning Disabled Children," *Journal of Learning Disabilities,* 1979, *12,* 487-491.

Vance, H. B., Wallbrown, F. H., & Blaha, J. "Determining WISC-R Profiles for Reading Disabled Children," *Journal of Learning Disabilities,* 1978, *11,* 657-661.

Wallbrown, F. H., & Blaha, J. "The Hierarchical Factor Structure of the WISC-R for Reading Disabled Children," *Multivariate Experimental Clinical Research,* 1979, *4*(3), 73-80.

Wallbrown, F. H., Blaha, J., & Vance, H. B. "A Reply to Miller's Concerns about WISC-R Profile Analysis," *Journal of Learning Disabilities,* 1980, *13,* 340-345.

Wallbrown, F. H., Vance, H. B., & Blaha, J. "Developing Remedial Hypotheses from Ability Profiles," *Journal of Learning Disabilities,* 1979, *12,* 557-561.

Wechsler, D. *Wechsler Intelligence Scale for Children: WISC Manual.* New York: Psychological Corporation, 1949.

Wechsler, D. *The Measurement and Appraisal of Adult Intelligence,* fourth edition. Baltimore: Williams & Wilkins, 1958.

Wechsler, D. *Wechsler Preschool and Primary Scale of Intelligence: WPPSI Manual.* New York: Psychological Corporation, 1967.

Wechsler, D. *Wechsler Intelligence Scale for Children—Revised: WISC-R Manual.* New York: Psychological Corporation, 1974.

Wechsler, D. *Wechsler Adult Intelligence Scale—Revised: WAIS-R Manual.* New York: Psychological Corporation, 1981.

Witkin, H. A., Dyk, R.B., Faterson, H.F., Goodenough, D.R., & Karp, S.A. *Psychological Differentiation.* New York: John Wiley, 1962.

Appendix A

WISC-R

RECORD FORM

Wechsler Intelligence Scale for Children—Revised

NAME __John__ AGE 10-1 SEX M

ADDRESS _____

PARENT'S NAME _____

SCHOOL _____ GRADE 3 _____

PLACE OF TESTING _____ TESTED BY Searls

REFERRED BY Classroom Teacher _____

WISC-R PROFILE

Clinicians who wish to draw a profile should first transfer the child's *scaled scores* to the row of boxes below. Then mark an X on the dot corresponding to the scaled score for each test, and draw a line connecting the X's.*

	Year	Month	Day
Date Tested	79	11	5
Date of Birth	69	10	5
Age	10	1	0

VERBAL TESTS / PERFORMANCE TESTS

Scaled Score boxes — Verbal: Information 7, Similarities 11, Arithmetic 7, Vocabulary 13, Comprehension 13, Digit Span 5

Scaled Score boxes — Performance: Picture Completion 16, Picture Arrangement 13, Block Design 15, Object Assembly 16, Coding 9, Mazes —

*See Chapter 4 in the manual for a discussion of the significance of differences between scores on the tests.

NOTES

	Raw Score	Scaled Score
VERBAL TESTS		
Information	11	7
Similarities	14	11
Arithmetic	9	7
Vocabulary	36	13
Comprehension	22	13
(Digit Span)	(7)	(5)
Verbal Score		51
PERFORMANCE TESTS		
Picture Completion	24	16
Picture Arrangement	32	13
Block Design	43	15
Object Assembly	28	16
Coding	38	9
(Mazes)	( )	( )
Performance Score		69

	Scaled Score	IQ
Verbal Score	51	101
Performance Score	69	128
Full Scale Score	120	114

*Prorated from 4 tests, if necessary.

Appendix B

WISC-R DATA SHEET

Name of Subject _____ Age _____ Date _____

Examiner _____ Sex _____ Grade _____

Full Scale IQ _____ Wechsler Classification of Intelligence

Verbal IQ _____ _____

Performance IQ _____ Difference between V and P IQS _____

SUBTEST SCALED SCORES

		Diff. from	Lower than
Verbal Scale		Scale Mean	Higher Mean
1. Information	_____	_____	_____
2. Similarities	_____	_____	_____
3. Arithmetic	_____	_____	_____
4. Vocabulary	_____	_____	_____
5. Comprehension	_____	_____	_____
6. Digit Span (Supplement)	_____	_____	_____
Sum of Verbal Tests	_____		
Verbal Mean	_____		
Performance Scale			
7. Picture Completion	_____	_____	_____
8. Picture Arrangement	_____	_____	_____
9. Block Design	_____	_____	_____
10. Object Assembly	_____	_____	_____
11. Coding	_____	_____	_____
12. Mazes (Supplement)	_____	_____	_____
Sum of Perf. Tests	_____		
Performance Mean	_____		

Appendix C

ABILITIES MEASURED BY TWO OR MORE WISC-R SUBTESTS

Name of Subject _____   Date _____

		Verbal Scale					Performance Scale					
Abilities	I	S	A	V	C	DS	PC	PA	BD	OA	Cod	Maz
a. Vis-Percep							—	—				
b. Vis-Mot-Coor											—	—
c. Vis-Mot-Spat									—	—		
d. Attention						—	—					
e. Att + Concen	—							—			—	
f. Concept Form	—	—	—	—	—			—				
g. Sch-Acq-Knowl	—		—	—								
h. Abst. Thought	—		—						—			
i. Sequencing						—		—			—	
j. Sch-Like Task	—											
k. Visualize Whole								—		—		
l. S-T Memory	—			—								—
m. L-T Memory	—	—		—	—							
n. Att to Details							—	—			—	
o. Environ-Exper.	—			—	—		—					

Note. I = Information, S = Similarities, A = Arithmetic, V = Vocabulary, C = Comprehension, DS = Digit Span, PC = Picture Completion, PA = Picture Arrangement, BD = Block Design, OA = Object Assembly, Cod = Coding, Maz = Mazes.